GRASPING
FOR POWER

GRASPING FOR POWER

Be Careful Who You Follow

ANGELA MARSHALL

ARCHWAY
PUBLISHING

Archway Publishing books may be ordered through booksellers or by contacting:

Archway Publishing
1663 Liberty Drive
Bloomington, IN 47403
www.archwaypublishing.com
844 669 3957

Because of the dynamic nature of the Internet, any web addresses or links contained in this book may have changed since publication and may no longer be valid. The views expressed in this work are solely those of the author and do not necessarily reflect the views of the publisher, and the publisher hereby disclaims any responsibility for them.

Any people depicted in stock imagery provided by Getty Images are models, and such images are being used for illustrative purposes only. Certain stock imagery © Getty Images.

ISBN: 978-1-6657-5071-4 (sc)
ISBN: 978-1-6657-5072-1 (e)

Library of Congress Control Number: 2023918784

Print information available on the last page.

Archway Publishing rev. date: 10/19/2023

Contents

Chapter – One

INTRODUCTION

November 10, 2004, the evening of the Annual Veterans Day Banquet. Each attendee entering the large auditorium was given a small United States Flag, which they held high and waved as they were being escorted to their table. Upon reaching her table, Angela was pleased to see that it was just below the stage and directly across from the head tables. That placed her in full view of the guest speaker. The speaker for the occasion was Lieutenant General Russel Honore, whom she had listened to daily during the horrible disasters caused by Hurricane Katrina and the flooding of the levee.

As she stood watching esteemed guests making their way to the head tables, she would occasionally catch the eye of someone she knew personally. In acknowledging their smile, she would twirl her flag high to say hello. After the head table guests were in and the invocation and singing of the National Anthem had ended, the attendees took their seats. Shortly afterward, the attendees at her table started introducing themselves. Angela was immediately taken by surprise upon seeing a former unit member whom she hadn't seen in more than eight years seated at the end. Hearing the two of them talk, it was easy to listen to the joy being expressed. One of the other attendees inquired as to how long they had known each other. Colonel Lister then took the opportunity to share with him, telling them that he and Angela were both retired members of the 87th Maneuver Area Command. He went on to say that it had been a while since they last talked.

Soon afterward, the waiters were placing the meals on the table. As they were eating, they started talking about General Honore and how he had handled the Katrina devastation.

Approximately an hour later, the program started when the master of the ceremony rose and started tapping on the podium to get the attention of the attendees. After the noise had ceased, he began introducing the head table guest. Introducing the forty-five distinguished guests with long, impressive titles took a while. Following his introductions, and a few other comments made by other speakers, the gentleman who was to present the speaker for the occasion came up to the podium. They had chosen an outstanding presenter, a man who was excellent in tone and pronunciation and had a great deal of enthusiasm in his voice. After his introduction, General Honore rose. As he stepped to the podium, the attendees stood and started applauding. Finally, the General began waving his hands, gesturing to the crowd to tone down. A short time later, the attendees took their seats, and General Honore started speaking. Throughout his presentation, attendees would stand and applaud upon hearing remarks they could personally relate to. Hearing General Honore in person was exhilarating from the beginning to the end. After his presentation, the master of the ceremony again stood and introduced another speaker. When the speaker started making his comments, quietness filled the large auditorium as he read excerpts from the biographical summaries of the men receiving awards. He spoke of their accomplishments and the battles they had fought and survived. Listening to his remarks, Angela's eyes became wet with tears, for she knew firsthand the damage the Vietnam (conflict) war had caused so many. During a phase of that war, Angela was stationed at the Marine Corps Air Facility on Okinawa, Japan. She had spent numerous hours sitting at the bedside of many wounded soldiers hospitalized at Camp Buckner, an Army Base hospital on the Island.

Following the presentations and throughout the remainder of the evening, the band performed. Each time the band played a song relating to the various branch(s) of the military service, current and former soldiers who had served in those branches would stand. Angela stood three different times because she had served in three separate components during her 23 years of military service: The US Marine Corps, the Alabama National Guard, and the US Army Reserves.

February 2007, twenty-seven months later, Angela is entering her second month of retirement after working twenty-six years, in the area her manuscript covers. Unlike many retirees, she was looking forward to starting two new careers; one in food services catering and one in writing. She was planning to expand her catering business, a small prosperous home-based business that had gotten her through many financial difficulties. She also wanted to finish a book she had started writing years earlier but had ceased writing because of job place issues she was having to contend with. Angela believed that telling her story of what she and two of the women had done to teach their cheating lover a lesson could benefit other men and women. However, both of those desires were being put on hold because a new objective had come about. She wanted to write a book about difficulties she had faced during a phase of her work history. Though she realized that many people have gone through similar situations, she still wanted to share her stories in hopes that others could learn and see how her faith in God enabled her to overcome those difficulties.

When watching television news, it's difficult to believe that people can do the most horrible things when confronted with problems they cannot handle. The characters in the story she wanted to write, demonstrated how weak and destructive some people can be when faced with disappointments.

April 2007, Angela awoke around 5:45 a.m. After going through her usual morning routine of prayer and Bible study, she went about the task of putting the trash bags out on the curbside. The bags were filled with shredded, work-related documents she had held on to for a number of years.

A short time later, after freshening up and preparing a cup of coffee, she was standing in her den, staring at storage containers filled with old documents. *'Three Counties signed resolutions to break away from the Planning Commission (PC)'* was the headline on a newspaper she had placed on the top of one of the containers. She picked up the newspaper and started reading the sections she had highlighted some years earlier. As she read, memories of those years began rushing through her mind. *She remembered* that the Commission staff had always believed that a division breakaway would never happen. Their belief was based on a statement made by the Commission's Executive Director, who was convinced that his executive committee would never allow the division to break away. As she placed the newspaper back on the pile, she smiled and said, *'Oh well, those county commissioners wished it had been that simple.'*

As she was preparing to go through the containers and sort through the documents, she placed all the items needed close to her chair. As time passed, she stayed busy organizing papers to be trashed, shredded, or used for references in her writing. Sometimes, she would take an opportunity to read through some of the documents before shredding them. Upon reading a card relating to her first five years of employment after graduating from college, *her memories* took her back to those former years and the people she had worked with. The experience she acquired during those years equipped her to be strong and steadfast when facing job difficulties.

After graduating from the University of Alabama in 1980, Angela was hired as a social worker serving senior citizens in Jefferson County. Her job was to work with the senior citizens throughout the county and ensure that their needs were taken care of. While working in the senior centers, she became acquainted with politicians throughout the county during the election year. They would come to the senior centers and talk to the seniors in hopes of gaining their votes.

During those months, Angela kept abreast of all the local and national political news. When she was in the centers, the seniors often treated her like a news reporter. They would ask questions to get her to expound on issues concerning things the political candidates had told them. She would take the time to listen to the senior citizens express their thoughts, concerns, and beliefs before expressing her opinion.

As she was going through the documents relating to those years, she would sometimes read many of them to determine which one she would keep for reference. When the documents she was planning to shred began to pile up, she would start shredding. When the shredder would get too hot and cease shredding, she would take the time to read old greeting cards, and letters and look at pictures. As she looked at pictures and read the cards, she would often pause and reflect on some of the occasions. Sometimes her thoughts and memories would linger longer on some of the events. As she read through a farewell card sent to her twenty-two years earlier, she laughed upon reading words expressed by former co-workers. Two of her former co-workers had written kind words. Maybe they felt guilty considering the lies they had told, *Angela thought*. As she was shredding the card, she picked up another card that had instructions written on it. The card had been given to her by one of her former co-workers. The instructions were: 'Never visit a client before reading the information in the client's folder.' Angela smiled when she began *thinking* about the situation the instructions were attempting to prepare her for.

Angela *recalled* she had been on the job less than six months before learning the lesson her co-worker had referred to. Angela's failure to follow the instructions had put her in a horrifying situation. She had visited a client who lived in a flea-infested hoarders' den. The client hadn't cleaned her house in twenty years or more. The client had allowed filth to accumulate because of an argument she had with her children after they failed to pick up behind themselves. The interview on that occasion had been very brief due to the physical irritations Angela was experiencing. After leaving the client's home and going to her car, Angela realized her clothes were covered with fleas. She immediately attempted to brush the fleas off but was unsuccessful. Seeing the many fleas on her, she was panic-stricken. She quickly got in her car and drove hurriedly to a friend's veterinary clinic. Angela remembered rushing in, having both hands up and screaming, telling the staff in the presence of many customers that she had visited a client who lived in a filthy flea-infected home. As Angela sat thinking about that situation, she began laughing as she placed the card on the pile to be shredded. As the evening was drawing near, Angela realized she had spent practically all day sorting through old documents.

Early the following morning, Angela was up and at it again, more determined than ever to finish the job. As she sat going through containers and reading old documents, her *memories drifted* back to those earlier years when she read a letter of promotion sent to her by the agency executive director. During the first four years of Angela's five-year employment with the agency, she thought highly of the agency executive director and greatly admired her accomplishments. Angela watched the director take federal and state-funded programs from other agencies and build a comprehensive, multipurpose organization serving the county's senior citizens. The organization was envied by many; the seniors could get all of their needs taken care of in one location. One of the agencies, she took programs from was the Planning Commission (PC). The Planning Commission was one of twelve in the state, their region covered six of the state's sixty-seven counties. Each of the twelve PCs administered many federal and state grants allocated to their region. The Title III Aging Programs were among those grants. That program came under the Area Agencies on Aging (AAA) Division. In the early 1980s, Ms. Henderson, Angela's boss decided to become an AAA Director serving Jefferson County. Knowing that the Planning Commission was the AAA for Jefferson County, Ms. Henderson had but one choice: to fight and take the aging services from under the Commission. Considering she had successfully taken programs from other agencies, she believed she would have no problems taking the Title III Program.

Ms. Henderson's failure to anticipate having to fight with the state's other eleven Planning Commissions Executive Directors created a problem for her. The other PC Directors' major concerns were two-fold; first, they did not wish to see the creation of another AAA; mainly because it would split state and federal dollars thirteen ways. Second, Ms. Henderson's success could lead their AAA Directors to believe they could pull from under the PC and set up a self-governing entity. That action would have resulted in the PC's losing out on millions of state and federal dollars. However, having the other PC Executive Directors speaking out against her efforts, Ms. Henderson did not retreat. Realizing that her major obstacle would be getting the federal government to de-designate the Planning Commission as AAA for Jefferson County, and designating her agency, made her fight more viciously. To accomplish her goal, she tried to prove that the local PC was not providing quality services to the county's senior citizens. However, the PC did not sit back and do nothing; they fought back. Losing Jefferson County, which was the largest of the six counties they served, would result in them losing out on millions of dollars.

Chapter – Two

REMINISCING - GOOD AND BAD TIMES

As time passed, the struggle to become an AAA became more difficult, so Ms. Henderson decided to bring out her trump card. One of the County Commissioners was said to be a family member. When Ms. Henderson was losing her battle, she went to him for help. Working on the inside, he was successful in getting the other county commissioners to concede and allowed Ms. Henderson to take the Title III Aging Program from the PC. This resulted in Ms. Henderson being designated as the thirteenth (13) AAA in the state.

After becoming AAA, Ms. Henderson began fighting more viciously, taking programs from other agencies. Newspapers throughout the state wrote articles about the battles that were going on. Articles written in the editorial columns had many viewing Ms. Henderson as a powerful woman. Upon reading an article about Ms. Henderson's accomplishments, you would never believe it when you saw her.

Ms. Henderson was a small-frame White female, with shoulder-length blond hair. She stood 5'7" tall, with her weight in proportion to her height. However, despite the many services she provided for the elderly, she was not a likable person, and she didn't get along with other professionals. She very seldom smiled except when she was plotting a devious action, such as taking a program from another agency.

During Angela's first twelve months of employment with the agency, Ms. Henderson was building an aging services agency. Like all the other employees, Angela was proud to see their agency growing and providing more services. The growth meant advancements and promotions for them, and Angela was among those who advanced quickly. Even though she benefitted, she became aware of the bitterness that followed. Ms. Henderson's negative reputation and how she was viewed by other agency administrators made it difficult for the Senior Services staff. When working in the field many of Ms. Henderson's adversaries thought that Senior Services staff was evaluating their services and programs to be taken over by Ms. Henderson.

When Ms. Henderson wanted to take a program, it was said, that she first made her case with state and local politicians. She invited them to every agency social gathering and showered them with praises. While making friends with the politicians, she created enemies among the agencies she was trying to take programs from. If you were operating a program that benefitted senior citizens and she wanted the program, she would smile, and tell you the program would be better managed under her administration.

Ms. Henderson was well-versed in knowing all the rules and regulations of the programs under her administration. However, being an AAA, she was prohibited from administering aging programs and services. To avoid being prohibited from serving the elderly, she formed a non-profit dummy holding corporation to receive and manage the federal and state funds that supported the programs she provided. During Angela's years of employment, the senior services came under the AAA had two directors: Ms. Sanders and later Ms. Adams.

Ms. Sanders, being the first, was a light brown complexion black woman, she had long black hair that she wore in a ponytail. Like Ms. Henderson, she was well-versed, knowing all the federal and state laws and guidelines governing the programs that came under the service agency. When Ms. Henderson was taking an action that Ms. Sanders knew was unquestionably wrong, Ms. Sanders would caution her. Whereas Ms. Sanders managed the programs according to federal and state guidelines, Ms. Henderson was always grasping for power, trying to show that it was her way or no way. She would operate under a course of action that met her desires. People around the county spoke of Ms. Sanders as a person with high ethical standards, but Ms. Henderson was regarded as a power-hungry woman. She acquired that label when she started downsizing other agencies by taking their programs.

As months went by, Ms. Sanders' opposing views of Ms. Henderson's decisions eventually resulted in Ms. Henderson's decision to get rid of her. However, Ms. Sanders did not sit back and do nothing; she filed an unfair dismissal lawsuit. When the case was going on, several staff members voiced their opinions about how Ms. Henderson had treated Ms. Sanders. Hearing of their disapproval of her actions, Ms. Henderson decided to get rid of them. However, being under scrutiny during that time, Ms. Henderson knew that dismissing another county employee would result in multiple lawsuits, so she put them under a great deal of stress, forcing them to resign. Though Ms. Henderson would never tell you to shun a staff member she was displeased with, she would give you plenty of clues, and your failure to get the message would result in your becoming her next target. The first person to go was Denise; a White female. Ms. Henderson began dumping loads of work on Denise and required her to complete the task in short periods. The workload is too much to bear resulting in Denise leaving. One day Denise went out on a break but never returned. The next day her mother and father came in and gathered all of her belongings and told several staff members what had happened.

After Denise left, the only two white males followed. Knowing how they felt about her actions, Ms. Henderson began imposing the same type of stress on them she had used on Denise. After tolerating as much as they were willing to put up with, they decided to resign and take another county position. One day, the two guys invited several staff members out for lunch. While having lunch they both announced that they were resigning.

Several months later, Ms. Sanders won her lawsuit and was reinstated in her former position. To show her disapproval, Ms. Henderson refused to allow Ms. Sanders to move back into her formal office. Ms. Sanders was assigned a smaller office across from Ms. Henderson, where Ms. Henderson could see nearly everything she did. In Ms. Sander's office were an old worn desk, a telephone, a chair, and piles of outdated newspapers. Daily, Ms. Henderson had Ms. Sanders read old newspapers and write reports. Ms. Henderson was determined to force Ms. Sanders out again, but Ms. Sanders was determined to hold on and see how low Ms. Henderson would stoop to get rid of her. Ms. Sanders came in daily with a big smile and purposely spoke to each staff member. She would then make her way to Ms. Henderson's office and cheerfully greet her and ask for her daily assignment.

Staff members who interacted with Ms. Sanders were taking a big chance of being Ms. Henderson's next target. Nevertheless, on days Ms. Henderson was out of the office they would walk by Ms. Sanders' office and wave like children at play. As months went by, seeing the stress the staff was having to endure and realizing Ms. Henderson would not pull back from her wrath, Ms. Sanders decided to accept another county position. Her leaving took some of the stress off the staff.

With Ms. Sanders now out of the way, Ms. Henderson thought she would be able to hire the person of her choice immediately. However, several staff members in the county personnel department could be equally as strong-willed as Ms. Henderson. They forced Ms. Henderson to go through the proper hiring procedures. They sent competent applicants for interviews knowing Ms. Henderson would not accept them.

Unlike times before, Ms. Henderson would hire the person she wanted under a temporary employment agreement until she could get the person through the county personnel system. However, the person she wanted to hire was unwilling to come in under those terms. That forced Ms. Henderson to have to wait and go through the proper procedures. Finally, after months had passed and many applicants had been interviewed and rejected, Ms. Henderson was allowed to hire Ms. Adams. Unfortunately, Ms. Adams was unaware of Ms. Henderson's disposition and the pressure she could inflict when she wanted something done her way.

Ms. Adams was a white female. She stood about 5'11" tall, with her weight in proportion to her height. She was a dark brunette with clusters of grey. She was also a very religious woman. It was obvious, she carried herself in a way that showed it. She had a friendly disposition and she was also very cheerful. When she was first hired, she came to work daily humming a beautiful spiritual song. However, after several months on the job, you could see the change in her disposition after she had met with Ms. Henderson. When talking to staff, whom she felt comfortable around, she always made it clear that she disapproved of some of Ms. Henderson's actions. But considering she had a daughter in college, she was willing to stay until her daughter had gotten her degree.

As Angela sat *reminiscing*, hours passed, and then suddenly, the telephone started ringing. Upon answering the phone and chatting for a brief period, she told her friend that she had been *reminiscing* about her years of employment working with senior citizens and how much she was able to learn being around them. As they talked, Angela told her friend that she had been holding onto containers of documents she would use for reference for the book she was planning to write. Angela went on to tell her friend that the documents were bringing back memories of both good and bad times. After they had talked for a while longer and said goodbye, Angela decided to take a break.

Hours later, Angela was at it again. As time passed, her *thoughts drifted* when she picked up a photo of her former co-workers. The picture had been taken in 1981, while Ms. Sanders was still with the agency. Angela remembered it was when Ms. Henderson had again gone to battle with the Commission to take the Title V Senior Employment Program (SEP). That program funded employment training for qualified older workers. Ms. Henderson's goal was to take all of the county slots, which would have resulted in the Planning Commission no longer serving the county's elderly population. Though the battle to take that program was equally as challenging, she partly succeeded. She then promoted Angela to serve as program director. This promotion elevated Angela to a level of management. In her new role, she worked closely with Ms. Henderson. Weekly she and Ms. Henderson would meet for a friendly chat, and Ms. Henderson would praise Angela with a cheerful look before making suggestions. Having been trained by the national office that funded the program, Angela knew that the national office would not have approved of Ms. Henderson's recommendations; still, Angela would smile and pretend as if the suggestions were great.

Like all the other programs Mr. Henderson had taken and put under the dummy corporation, the Senior Employment Program was shown as a service offered by Senior Services. All of the program enrollees were hired under a contract with the dummy corporation. Angela would frequently interact with the corporation officers, the president, the vice president, and the secretary/treasurer. They were intelligent, well-educated, retired professionals in their late seventies and early eighties. Angela would meet with them for the signing of payroll checks and other documents. During those meetings, she would provide them with a friendly briefing on what they would say if ever asked questions about their roles and responsibilities. Angela also kept them informed about issues they were reading about in the newspapers, the great things Ms. Henderson was doing, and how much better off the programs were under Ms. Henderson's organization.

As time passed, everything seemed to have been going well. The senior workers enjoyed their jobs, and the host agency supervisors were pleased with the seniors. When the host agency supervisors would send Angela letters praising the workers' performance, Angela would send a copy to the national granting agency.

Yearly, the granting agency would send a representative down to monitor the program and review all the records to ensure federal compliance. The monitor's standard procedure was to meet with the contracting agency before proceeding with their monitoring. The representative would proceed to go through all the personnel and financial records, then follow up by visiting the agencies the senior workers were assigned for training. These agencies were referred to as host agencies. The purpose of the visits was to see the senior workers performing assigned tasks and to talk with the host agency administrators to ensure they understood the purpose of the program. Typically, this would take three to four days, depending on the region it covered and the number of senior workers. After the monitor had completed the work, they would conduct an exit visit with the agency administrator to discuss the findings, praise them for their accomplishments, and make recommendations.

When Ms. Adams was notified of the upcoming monitoring visit, she was pleased and confident that everything would go well. The agency had been monitored before, and they had gotten outstanding overall performance appraisals, and they expected no less. However, no one had anticipated the problem brought on when the national office sent down a different monitor.

The monitor was an older white gentleman. He had been with the national agency for a number of years and was seasoned in the role he was performing. Being his first visit, he followed all the standard operating procedures. In light of the fact he, too, was a retired military man, he and Angela immediately hit it off. After Mr. Mason and Angela had spent time talking, Angela took him to meet with Ms. Adams. After he and Ms. Adams had chatted for a while, Angela showed him around and provided him with a working space. The following morning, considering it was a beautiful day, Angela suggested spending some time in the field. Later that morning, the two left the office and headed to the field to visit several participating host agencies. The first two days went off well; however, what happened on the third day was not anticipated.

Chapter – Three

VALUABLE LESSONS LEARNED

H aving spent a portion of the second day visiting host agencies, Mr. Mason decided that he wanted to go out again and visit some of the other host agencies. As Mr. Mason was driving down the main street approaching the block the county courthouse was in, he decided it would be an excellent opportunity to stop in and talk with the county commissioner who signed off on the Senior Employment Service contract. It just so happened that a driver was pulling out of a parking space.

"This is what I call luck," Mr. Mason said. *"I'll pull in this space, and we can go in and talk to the commissioner."*

His statement caught Angela by surprise. Visiting the county commissioner had never been done before, so Angela immediately tried to talk him into going ahead with the host agency monitoring. But he was determined to go in and meet the local sponsor. Mr. Mason told Angela that he needed to talk to the county commissioner to ensure that the Commissioner clearly understood the purpose of the program. Angela knew that the county commissioner's only knowledge of the program was what he might have read about in the newspapers. He had little to no knowledge of the federal guidelines. On several occasions, Angela had taken the proposals and budgets to the commissioner, and he had signed off where indicated.

When Angela and Mr. Mason entered the courthouse, Angela immediately excused herself, telling him she needed to go to the ladies' room. But the fact was, she wanted to find a telephone booth so she could call Ms. Henderson and make her aware of their visit to the commissioner's office. Upon walking away, Angela assumed Mr. Mason would wait for her to return before going into the commissioner's office. However, to her surprise, upon returning, she saw that he had gone ahead and was talking with the commissioner's secretary. When the secretary told him the commissioner was out, Mr. Mason decided that he and Angela would wait for the commissioner to return. As they sat waiting, he and the secretary talked about things going on in the city. Mr. Mason and the secretary enjoyed talking so much, time slipped by. However, during their conversation, the commissioner called in and told the secretary he would not be coming back to the office that evening. It was at that point Mr. Mason and Angela left.

After they had finished their monitoring visits and returned to the office, Ms. Henderson's secretary called and told Angela that Ms. Henderson wanted to see the two of them. Knowing Ms. Henderson as Angela did, she and Mr. Mason went directly to Ms. Henderson's office. When they entered, Ms. Henderson started accusing Angela of going over her head by taking Mr. Mason to the county commissioner. Mr. Mason immediately came to Angela's defense, explaining that it was his decision. He further stated that he had an obligation to meet with the county commissioner to whom his agency had given hundreds of thousands of dollars. He then told Ms. Henderson that the national office required him to visit the grant recipients to ensure they fully understood the guidelines. As he talked, Angela sat quietly, listening as he attempted to resolve the misconception of the purpose of his visit. The more he spoke, the more Angela realized his explanations were being ignored. Angela was aware of Ms. Henderson's strategies and the pain she had inflicted on others, but she had never been a victim. This time, Mr. Mason was the primary victim, and he had no perception of what was to come. He had little to no knowledge of Ms. Henderson's personality and how forceful she could be in battle. During their discussion, a heated dispute commenced, centered on the guidelines Angela operated under. As the discussion continued, the two became more combative. Mr. Mason then thought he could intimidate Ms. Henderson by telling her he would recommend withdrawing the grant and giving the program back to the Planning Commission. However, Ms. Henderson was not intimidated by his threat. She took his threatening statement as a challenge and told him she would take the city slots from the Commission to prove who was in control. Ms. Henderson then ended the discussion by saying nothing more. She simply started dealing with the papers on her desk. Seeing that she was paying him no attention, he nodded at Angela, indicating they were to leave.

The following day Mr. Mason did not return to continue his monitoring. He decided to spend the morning in his hotel room making telephone calls to get information on Ms. Henderson. The information he was able to obtain was very discouraging yet enlightening. He learned from various reliable sources that the national office would not be able to take the program because Ms. Henderson had friends in powerful positions. Further, all of her paperwork was in order.

As time passed, Angela remained the program director. She continued performing excellently in all areas, but her relationship with Ms. Henderson had changed. They were no longer having their evening chats.

One afternoon after being in Ms. Henderson's office for a much longer period than usual, Ms. Adams came out and went directly to her office and closed her door. Several staff members who had seen her stated that she appeared very upset. Later that evening, Ms. Adams called Angela and told her they needed to talk. Angela immediately stopped what she was doing and went to Ms. Adams's office. Upon entering, Ms. Adams asked Angela to close the door and take a seat. While Angela sat quietly, waiting for Ms. Adams to say something, Ms. Adams sat with a distressed look. She began shaking her head and saying, *"I cannot believe this. I hate we have come to this point."*

"What are you referring to?" Angela asked.

"Ms. Henderson wants you back in the social worker's position."

"The social worker's position or out of the agency?"

"There was nothing I could say to change her mind. You're doing an excellent job, but you're now on her shit list for some unknown reason."

"Wow! What did I do?" Angela asked in a surprised tone.

"Nothing, but something or someone has pissed Ms. Henderson off."

Angela then asked Ms. Adams if she thought Ms. Henderson was still upset about her run-in with Mr. Mason nine months earlier. Ms. Adams told her that she was unsure about what had set Ms. Henderson off. She then reminded Angela that they both knew Ms. Henderson could hold a grudge for years. As they continued talking, Ms. Adams told Angela that Mr. Mason had a right to visit the county commissioner. As Ms. Adams spoke, her eyes became watery; she reached into her tissue box and pulled several tissues out to wipe away her tears. As she continued talking, she told Angela that she couldn't fight with Ms. Henderson because she was a widow with a child in college. Angela then got up and went around to comfort her and take the pressure off her by telling her she would be okay.

"I have other options," Angela said.

"I know you have. You have your catering business, and you're good at it, and I know you could go full-time with the military if you wanted to."

As they continued talking, though it was not said, the expression on Ms. Adams's face left Angela with the impression that it was time for her to seek employment elsewhere.

Ms. Henderson was known for trying to destroy a person she believed had not shown absolute loyalty to her. Perhaps based on her untrusting nature she believed that everyone else was disloyal.

Two weeks later, Angela moved back into her former role as one of the agency's social workers. Considering she did not have to take a salary cut, she was relatively content. During the nearly four years she served as Senior Employment Program Director, she faced many obstacles and bent many federal guidelines. However, knowing Ms. Henderson as she did, Angela knew it was only a matter of time before Ms. Henderson would get upset about something else she did or said.

Throughout the week, Angela and Ms. Adams jog together during their lunch break. On those occasions, Ms. Adams always said something that led Angela to decide it was now time to leave. After praying about her situation, Angela prepared a letter stating that she was resigning to pursue a long-desired dream.

Angela thought this was an excellent time to start working toward finishing a book she had started writing years earlier. During her last week of employment, Angela talked about the fun she would have fishing and writing. She owned a time-share condominium at Alpine Bay Resort and would often go up on weekends and do some fishing. When the information about Angela's plans got back to Ms. Henderson, she got the assistance of two of Angela's co-workers to lie about how Angela treated them. Both women stated that Angela was not cooperative in working with them, and her behavior hindered them from getting their jobs done. Ms. Henderson then took the time to go back and recall and re-write Angela's last job performance evaluation. Her actions were designed to prevent Angela from collecting vacation leave pay. In rewriting Angela's performance evaluation, she lowered the points one short of the limit required to collect vacation pay. Her steps were so despicable that several county employees in the personnel department went to their boss and complained. Seeing their boss was not going to do anything, the women got together, called Angela in, and encouraged her to protest the changes. As a single mother and knowing what money she had to live on, Angela decided not to fight with Ms. Henderson as Ms. Sanders had. Walking out of the courthouse Angela's mind was focused on the words written in *Jeremiah 29:11- For I know the thoughts that I think toward you declared the LORD, thoughts of peace and not of evil, to give you a future and a hope.*

After being unemployed for one week, Angela sent out three job applications. Two weeks later, she was called and offered a job with the Planning Commission. The offer came as a big surprise, for she had not submitted a job application to the Commission. As faith would have it, accepting the job would put her in control of the Commission Senior

Employment Program, the same program Ms. Henderson had taken slots from four years earlier and was contemplating fighting to take the slots allocated for the City of Birmingham.

Angela was excited about the job offer but unsure why Mr. Percy, the Executive Director, had offered the job to her. To better understand what was going on, she called Mr. Mason to see if he would fill her in on the details. She learned that the national office was putting pressure on Mr. Percy because the Commission was not meeting its minimum performance standards and was in jeopardy of losing its program. Mr. Mason told her that the program director frequently disregarded the rules and regulations. He encouraged Angela to go ahead and send in a copy of her resume. Mr. Mason told her that, the national office staff all believed that if anyone could solve the Commission compliance problems it would be her. He explained that even before she left the Senior Services Agency several staff members had highly recommended her for the position.

Angela was happy to learn that the national staff thought so highly of her job performance and ability to perform under pressure. Mr. Mason also told her that he had spoken with several people around the state, and they had told him that Ms. Henderson was extremely vindictive and would try to destroy anyone she believed was not loyal to her.

He then started telling her about some of the benefits to motivate Angela to take the job. He told her she would drive a company car, have several office spaces, and have a support staff. She would also have membership in the state retirement system and make several thousand dollars more than she had made with Senior Services. As they talked, he did not hold back on providing her with details about the program's condition. He admitted that he had been negligent in holding the PC SEP Director accountable; he gave her all the details about the host agency administrators, the senior workers, and the former SEP Director.

Angela then stated with a short chuckle. *"Sounds like I may be getting in a situation worse than the one I just left."*

"No, I don't think so. I know you can handle any problem you run into at the PC."

Chapter – Four

JOB CHANGE

September 5, 1985, Angela got up and went about the morning performing her routine tasks. This would be her first day at her new job. Wanting to make an impression, she selected a two-piece navy blue tailored business suit, a dusty rose-colored blouse, and a pair of navy blue heels. Standing in front of her mirror, putting makeup on, she realized how blessed she was. She smiled and thanked God as she remembered the words written in *Romans 8:28, "and we know that all things work together for good to those who love God, to those who are called according to His purposes."*

'I wonder what Ms. Henderson will think when she realizes she hasn't destroyed my chance for moving on.' *Angela thought.*

Thirty minutes later, Angela pulled into a parking space at the Park Building. When she entered the Planning Commission reception area, the receptionist paged Mr. Percy to let him know she had arrived. The secretary then escorted Angela to Mr. Percy's office to wait for his return. As Angela sat waiting, her attention was drawn to the pictures on his walls. She could see he was a nice-looking dark-completion White male with a full head of dark brown hair. From viewing the pictures of him standing with people she knew, she determined his height and weight to be about 5'11". As she looked around in his office, it was apparent that he liked documenting and showing off his professional achievements. He had pictures of himself with many well-known people in the aging network. All four walls, excluding the windows and door, were covered from the ceiling to the floor with pictures of him and other people he considered important. Unlike many people, who like taking pictures with different positions and facial expressions, each photo had the same pose and facial expression. After viewing all the pictures she could easily see, without getting up and freely moving around in his office, she looked down the hall and saw him approaching.

When Mr. Percy walked in, Angela stood. After exchanging brief greetings, she made flattering comments about several of the pictures. Angela was then taken by surprise when he started giving detailed information about many of the photographs. Listening to his remarks, she smiled and showed interest. On several occasions, she asked questions about the various sceneries captured in the photographs. After talking for nearly an hour, his secretary called and reminded him that the time for the management staff meeting was approaching. At that moment, he took out Angela's application and started asking questions. Angela had only held three full-time jobs and several part-time jobs. She had served three years of active duty in the United Marine Corps, four years with the Dallas County Department of Pension and Security, and four years with the New Vaughn Memorial Hospital Business Department. Angela had spent four years with the Alabama National Guard and five years with the US Army Reserves. She had also held several part-time jobs during her years of college. In addition to those skills, Angela possessed several talents and operated a small catering business. Despite her limited work history in the aging network, Mr. Percy was most impressed with the number of awards and certificates she had received for achievements and the services she had rendered. After discussing her past work experience, they headed to the conference room, where the management team was waiting.

The first person she met was David, the deputy director. David was

Mr. Percy's rival. Angela would later learn that David had applied for the executive director's position, but Mr. Percy had been chosen. This led to a battle between the two men, which had gone on for several years.

David was a tall, medium-built, attractive White male with dark brown hair. He stood approximately 6'2", with his weight in proportion to his height. He was extremely friendly, and Angela immediately felt comfortable in his presence. The next person who approached her was the Transportation Division Director. Blair was a tall, slim White male; he stood approximately 6'4" and weighed about 210 lbs. Blair had dark brown shoulder-length curly hair and a full beard. The next person she met was the Director of Governmental Services and Special Projects, a short chubby White male. He stood approximately 5'4" and weighed about 250 lbs. It was obvious, he liked eating; his belly would give you the impression that he was carrying twins. One after the other, the male division directors would introduce themselves. The last person to approach Angela was Susan, the Area Agency on Aging, Director and rival of Ms. Henderson.

Susan was an attractive White female, approximately 5'9" tall, with a slim physique. She weighed no more than 135 lbs. She styled her auburn color hair, with streaks of gray flowing down her back.

After meeting each division director, Angela was given a briefing about the Planning Commission Board. The board consisted of one hundred members: the mayors, probate judges, and county commissioners from the townships of the six counties the PC served. Nineteen of the 100 members served on the executive committee. These members established policies for finance, personnel hiring, dismissal, programs, services provided, and management issues. After she had been given details about the agency's functions, the management team started questioning Angela. They all seemed very interested in her work experience with Ms. Henderson. Each took term asking questions, but Angela would only answer when the question seemed appropriate. She told the team she did not feel it was necessary to discuss Ms. Henderson's personality, considering much of what Ms. Henderson did or said was covered in the newspapers.

After the management team meeting, Angela was escorted through the departments and introduced to the other staff members who worked with the division directors. Later that morning, after meeting with all the Commission staff, Angela settled in her office and got busy with her job duties.

Angela was hired to clean up the Senior Employment Program and administer several small employment services contracts. But first, she needed to unscramble the puzzle she had been given. Mr. Mason had briefed her about the many problems she would face. She was also aware that she needed to resolve the issues before the end of the contract year, which was ten months away. Solving the problems was like going on an expedition without a map, but Angela was confident she could solve all of the issues in the time frame required. She believed in an old saying, 'Follow the money trail.' It was not that the former director did not create personnel, administrative, and monetary records; the problem was she failed to organize and maintain the records. Sorting through the papers was like putting a thousand-piece puzzle together without a good picture.

Angela's first two weeks on the job were very hectic. In addition to sorting through the records, she was going out meeting and establishing relationships with participating host agency administrators and community leaders. The area she had to cover extended over five counties, and the City of Birmingham.

When she was in the office, she frequently got telephone calls from people who wanted to talk about Ms. Henderson. But Angela believed in, and tried to practice the words written in *Philippians 3:13-14, I do not count myself to have apprehended; but one thing I do, forgetting those things which are behind and reaching forward to those things which are ahead."*

One afternoon three weeks after being hired, Angela was surprised when three of her former co-workers stopped by to bring a gift. As Angela read the card, she was surprised to see that all the staff, including Ms. Henderson and the two women who had told lies about her, had signed the greeting card and made warm comments. Angela then picked up the beautifully wrapped gift and placed it on her desk. In a teasing manner, she stared at the package as her former co-workers stood eagerly waiting to see the expression on her face when she saw the gift. To Angela's amazement, it was a silver serving coffee set.

"I can't believe this," she said, *"whose idea was this?"*

"We all decided to vote on the various suggestions," Miranda said.

Angela's former co-workers were aware of her love for silver serving pieces. Each time they had an office party, Angela always brought out her fine silver pieces for the occasion.

"Thank you; I love it. This is just what I need."

"I told y'all she would say that," Laura said to Joanna and Miranda.

After talking for a brief period, Angela thanked them with an embrace and walked with them to the elevator. After returning to her office, she closed the door and got busy reviewing personnel files.

Several days later, shortly after getting to work, the florist delivered a dozen long-stem red roses. Later that morning, the gentleman Angela was dating came to see her. When he announced himself to the secretary, the secretary was surprised upon hearing him say, *"Tell her it's Judge."*

He then inquired as to which office Angela was in and asked if he could surprise her. The secretary escorted him to Angela's office, knocked on the door, stood back, and allowed him to enter. Upon entering, he embraced Angela as he closed the door with his foot. After spending a few moments behind closed doors talking, Angela walked with him to the lobby, embraced him with a kiss, and said goodbye.

He was a tall, handsome fellow with his weight in proportion to his height. He had a chestnut brown complexion. He was also a show-off, always wearing good-looking professionally tailored suits. He was a man with various talents; in addition to his job as an engineer, he and Angela were known around town for conducting motivational training seminars.

Shortly after he had left, several of Angela's co-workers who had seen him began inquiring after the secretary had gone around whispering about him. His name was not commonly given to male baby boys in those days, so the staff assumed he was a justice of the peace. Knowing what they were thinking, Angela chose not to correct them.

As she worked, it was difficult for her to concentrate while standing at the file cabinet where she had placed the vase of roses. She smiled when she remembered a former military dinner they had attended several months earlier. The affair was held at Green Valley Country Club. Their seating place cards read; Master Sergeant Angela Marshall and, of course, Judge Johnson. Despite the many VIPs attending the prestigious affair, much attention was focused on Angela and her guest. Everyone wanted to know more about the handsome gentleman escorting her. Other guests would come over for a brief chat to get information about him. As Angela stood at the file cabinet thinking about things that had occurred that evening, a page from a folder she was reviewing fell to the floor, disrupting her thoughts. Upon regaining her attentiveness, she picked up the paper and continued to go through the folders.

Hours later, shortly after 8:00 p.m., having spent most of the day reviewing personnel and fiscal records, Angela decided to call it a day. Angela worked an average of twelve hours daily striving to solve the problems.

The following day Angela started her mornings in the field visiting host agencies; her first visit was to the local Red Cross. During a conversation with one of the supervisors, Angela was utterly surprised upon learning what one of the senior workers assigned to the agency was doing. The supervisor praised the work of the 86-year-old homebound, physically disabled White female. This senior worker worked out of her home, making small clothing for newborn babies and disadvantaged small children. Working out of her home was considered non-compliant under federal guidelines. The former program director had allowed this to go on for more than eight years. As the supervisor continued praising the worker, Angela did not display her disapproval. After leaving the agency, Angela went directly to the senior's home; it was apparent the supervisor had called and told the senior worker Angela would be coming by. Upon entering, Pearl, the senior, cheerfully greeted Angela with a warm embrace and then offered her a cup of coffee. As they sat chatting, Pearl began showing Angela copies of newspaper articles with pictures of her giving clothing gifts to mothers for their newborns. Over the years, Pearl had received numerous thank-you cards from families and hospital staff, and she wanted Angela to read many of them. As she rolled around in her wheelchair, gathering things to show Angela, Angela was deeply moved. However, she knew she could not allow Pearl to remain on the program working out of her home. Finally, after Angela had acquired all the information she needed, she took pictures of Pearl before departing. After getting in her car, she sat silently, praying and asking God for guidance. Not wanting Pearl to wonder why she was still parked in the drive, Angela drove to a nearby park and sat in her car, praying about the situation.

As she went through another folder, she realized the host agency the senior worker was assigned to work at was nearby, but when she went into the agency and inquired about the senior worker, no one knew the lady. Thinking that maybe she had misread the information in the folder, she took a moment to review all the necessary forms. Looking through the folder, she could see that the documents were misleading. The records showed that the senior was assigned to fill a position the agency had no need for. Using the agency telephone, Angela dialed the telephone number shown in the folder. When the lady answered, Angela was delighted to hear her voice and know she was a real person, not a fictitious name. After announcing who she was, Hannah, the senior, invited Angela to stop off at her home for a visit. Listening to the instructions, Angela could understand why Hannah had been given the assignment as a transportation aide. Her ability to provide detailed directions was remarkable. Angela was able to follow the directions without any difficulties. Upon arriving, Hannah warmly greeted Angela and offered her a glass of iced tea. The two then sat on the screened-in porch, chatting.

Angela was amazed; Hannah was a young-looking, attractive 76-year-old Black female. She was a small-frame woman with long grey hair that hung down her back. As they talked, Angela was amazed to learn that, besides transporting seniors around, Hannah taught swimming lessons to senior citizens three days a week at the local YWCA. After Angela had acquired all the information she needed, she took a photo of Hannah before leaving.

Though Angela did not intend to spend her time visiting senior workers in their homes, she would later find herself during that. Angela needed to see these individuals in person, performing the job the paperwork stated they had been hired to perform.

As she was driving back to the office, she thought about how she would resolve the two problems she had just discovered. Considering the two women were performing a valuable mission and helping so many people, Angela felt she could not abruptly bring these services to an end. On her way back to the office Angela prayed asking for God's guidance and her ability to make the best decision, *Psalm 25:4-5, Show me your way, Lord, show me the paths and guide me....*

Chapter – Five

PROBLEMS-SOLVING

The following week, Angela made numerous telephone calls to find suitable host agency placements for the two ladies. After some persuasive talks, she successfully got the Red Cross Administrator to set up space so Pearl could come in and do her sewing. Learning that a local church sponsored a program that met the federal requirements, Angela met with the pastor and got him to agree to become a host agency. Upon learning that the church van driver was age and income-eligible, she enrolled the gentleman in the program. Hannah was then assigned as a transportation aide, traveling on the van. Pearl was picked up three days weekly and transported to and from the Red Cross building. She was no longer shut up in her home alone. Getting out and being with other people significantly lifted her spirit. People would visit her at the Red Cross building and assist her.

After reading a newspaper article highlighting the wonderful job, Pearl was doing, one of the local Hancock Fabrics stores started giving Pearl fabrics and other items needed to make clothing for needy small children and newborns. With the changes, Pearl was performing the same task, on a larger scale and being aided and supervised.

Having the church sign up as a host agency using their van to transport seniors around, aided many elderly citizens. They were transported to and from medical appointments, drug stores, grocery stores, general shopping excursions, and nursing homes to visit family and friends.

To advertise the program, Angela provided Hannah and Pearl with a monogrammed jacket, writing pens, and business cards that contained basic marketing information.

In an interview with newspaper reporters, Pearl and Hannah praised the national program and talked about their wages and how the extra money had enhanced their lives and standard of living. When questioned about Angela and the changes she was making, they told the reporters that Angela was putting into practice the program guidelines, which had always been there, just never enforced. Angela was extremely pleased by the things the two women had said. She was hoping their comments about the changes would make other senior workers facing changes more at ease. However, a few seniors were determined to cause problems. They wrote letters and a few called their congressman and complained. They said they had been with their current host agency for six to eight years, and the former director had never tried to move them around. When Angela got calls from the members of Congress, she would provide them with the necessary documents, which explained the program guidelines. In addition, Angela sent them copies of newspaper articles about senior workers who had made the transitions. After the Congressman had reviewed the guidelines, they would send letters commending Angela.

Weekly, Angela sent copies of newspaper articles to the national office showing the positive changes she was making and the positive things many seniors were saying. The national office was extremely pleased to see that Angela had solved many problems and had received positive public feedback.

After having been on the job for less than a hundred days, Angela had solved all of the significant compliance problems that put the Commission at risk of losing the program. With the compliance problems solved, Angela continued working long hours trying to find jobs for the seniors who could leave the program and go into unsubsidized jobs before the end of the program year.

With the major issues behind her, Angela had more time to get better acquainted with the Commission staff. Occasionally Angela and Susan would arrive in the parking lot around the same time. When Angela wasn't in a hurry, she would wait while Susan gathered her daily supplies; a large glass jar with a handle, a sack of lemons or lines, her briefcase, and an oversized purse. One morning Angela took the time to wait and walk in with Susan.

As they got in the elevator, Susan told Angela she had gotten an invitation to a reception at the New Ramada Inn. She then inquired, asking Angela if she had received one. When Angela told her that she did not get an invitation, Susan invited Angela to join her.

Susan then started telling Angela about some of the problems that were going on in their counties. In addition to the problems, she told Angela that two of the county aging program coordinators were asking for more money so they could make financial contributions to the Senior Employment Program. She asked Angela why the money was needed. Angela was surprised that the former program director had never spoken to Susan about the required 10% non-federal matching funds. Angela then explained that the national office did not provide administrative operating costs. She said that each project was responsible for its own administrative expenses. That statement got Susan's attention, and she wanted to know how Angela got her administrative funds.

Angela proceeded to tell Susan how she was able to raise the money. She told her that the 10% non-federal matching portion was contributed by the host agencies that trained the workers assigned to them. She explained in detail all the expenses the non-federal portion covered, which included salary, fringe, in-direct costs, some of her office equipment, and special supplies.

"*I was unaware of that,*" Susan told her. "*You must raise a sizable amount.*"

"*I do; the host agencies understand, considering all the expenses of the workers are covered by the national office.*"

After having talked about a few other issues they departed and Angela proceeded to her office.

Later that evening after finishing the contracts she was planning to take to the State Welfare Agency the next day, Angela made her way to the Ramada Inn to meet Susan. When she arrived, she made her way through the crowded room to the bar area, where Susan was chatting with two guys.

"Hi, girl!" Susan cheerfully greeted Angela. *"I'm glad you made it. Let me introduce you to two of my friends."*

She then proceeded to introduce Angela to Jeff and Dale. She told the two men that she and Angela worked together. Then excitedly added, telling them that Angela was a US Marine.

"You don't say," Dale commented. *"I have never had the pleasure of shaking hands with a woman Marine."*

Angela smiled, *"Once a Marine, you're always a Marine."*

Jeff then signals the waiter to come over and take their orders. He suggested that Angela go over and get some cocktail snacks before they were all gone.

"Try the crab cakes," Jeff said as Susan and Angela walked away.

As the two guys were looking around, Dale noticed that the busboy was cleaning off a table. They hurriedly went over and took possession of the table, and waved to Susan and Angela. When Angela and Susan joined them, the four sat chatting and laughing about various things, but mostly Alabama politics.

Dale and Jeff were good-looking White men who appeared to be in their late thirties to the early '40s. They were about the same height, and their weight was proportional to their size. Dale was a dark brunette, and Jeff was a light auburn. They both wore their hair cut short and neatly trimmed.

As the four sat talking, it became apparent that Susan had started focusing her attention elsewhere. Seeing that she was looking toward the bar, Dale inquired, asking her if she knew the guy looking in their direction.

"I'm not sure," Susan said, *"He's looking over here, but I don't recognize him."*

Susan then gestured, inviting the guy to come over. When he approached the table and introduced himself as Bruce Walker, Angela looked and realized he was someone she knew.

Bruce was a good-looking White male, about six feet tall, with his weight in proportion to his height. He wore his coffee brown hair neatly cut and trimmed.

"Wow, you look great," Bruce told Angela.

Angela smiled and returned the compliment; *"And so do you. Would you believe I didn't recognize you in your civilian attire?"* She said.

"So you know each other," Dale said.

"We do," Bruce told them.

That evening, Bruce was wearing a black three-piece pin-stripe suit with a white shirt and a black and white paisley necktie. As Angela admired his suit, she complimented him on the style, for she was not accustomed to seeing him in civilian attire. During their drill weekends, he and Angela were always dressed in their battle dress uniform (BDU).

For a brief moment, Bruce and Angela chatted as the three looked on, and then suddenly, they were interrupted when Susan started tapping on her glass to get their attention. Bruce apologized, telling them that he and Angela were in the 87th Maneuver Area Command but hadn't seen each other in a while.

"Hum," Dale said, *"Susan, you didn't tell us Angela was still in the military."*

"What rank are you?" Susan asked.

"Major."

"Well... join us; I'm Susan, this is Dale, and he's Jeff."

Dale and Jeff told Bruce that they were both Delta Airline Pilots. Susan interrupted and told Bruce she was a former flight attendant who had flown with the two.

"That must have been a rewarding job. What do you do now?" Bruce asked.

"Triple-A Director."

For a brief moment, Bruce appeared as if he wanted to ask another question. Seeing the expression on his face, Angela smiled and said, *"No, neither of those. Susan is the Area Agency on Aging, Director, acronyms AAA. We both work for the Planning Commission."*

"Okay." Bruce smiled and said.

The four started chuckling upon becoming aware of what Bruce may have been thinking.

"You have to be clear when using acronyms," Dale said.

A short time later, after they had gotten comfortable, they started chatting about things happening around the world. Then, one of them brought up the subject of Alabama politics. That started a discussion that went on for a while. They each expressed their feeling about the fight that was going on between Attorney General Greyson and Lieutenant Booker, two democrats running for state governor.

As they talked, expressing their thoughts, it was apparent they were enjoying each other's company from their laughter. As time passed and the atmosphere began to change, Susan suggested they go up the hill to Cheers, another popular evening venue with a similar atmosphere.

Cheers' sat on a high heel and the bar provided a more spectacular view of the surrounding area. The scenery and soft piano music attracted many professional couples between 9:30 p.m. and 1:00 a.m. Upon entering Cheers Bar, they were able to get a table near a window overlooking the City of Birmingham. After they had ordered drinks, they resumed their conversation about Alabama Politics.

Shortly after midnight, Bruce announced that he had a busy day planned and needed to get on the road. The three men then stood, shook hands, and said goodbye. Thirty minutes after Bruce had left, Angela decided she needed to say goodbye. She informed them that she needed to be in Montgomery early to deliver some contracts. But before leaving, In light of the fact they had such a great time socializing together, they made plans to get together the next time Dale and Jeff were in town.

The following day after returning from Montgomery, Angela stopped in Susan's office to thank her for the wonderful evening. They chatted briefly about things that had gone on. Susan told Angela that she had made a great impression on Dale and Jeff, and they were looking forward to our next outing. Susan then inquired about Bruce's marital status. From the questions asked and the things she said, it was apparent to Angela that Susan was interested in getting hooked up with Bruce.

Shortly after Angela entered her office, she was approached by Camilla, Susan's assistant. Camilla had overheard part of the conversation between Angela and Susan, and she wanted to know if Angela would join her and Lynette for lunch.

Several hours later, the three were having lunch together. After they had chatted for a few minutes, Camilla and Lynette started inquiring about Angela's evening with Susan, they wanted to know if Susan had told her about the aging program's problems. Angela informed them that she and Susan did not talk about work-related issues.

"Hum," Lynette commented as she looked at Camilla. *"Well,"* she said, *"We just as well tell you because you're bound to hear from other sources."*

Lynette and Camilla then started telling Angela that several Scott County officials were trying to gain support to pull the aging program from under the Commission. The two further explained that Scott County officials had tried to pull away years earlier. However, they had recently learned that the Woodrow County Aging Program Coordinator was talking about joining forces with Scott County. As Angela listened, she could sense that they were deeply concerned. Angela then inquired as to why Scott and Woodrow County Coordinators wanted to pull away. They told her that in addition to wanting to be independent, they both wanted more of the federal and state dollars the Commission was getting for the five counties. Being somewhat knowledgeable about federal funding, Angela told them that if the Title III grant was awarded based on the same factors as the Title V grant, the two counties would not get any more money.

"You may be right," Camilla said, *"but they think they will."*

"Oh well," Angela commented. *"It's always the money."*

As they continued talking, Lynette told Angela that the two county coordinators believed that Susan could give them more money if she didn't have to pay so much in-direct cost.

Angela chuckled: *"How do they know how much she pays?"*

"They know," Camilla said.

"Angela…, if you hear anything, you'll let us know, won't you?" Lynette said.

"Of course, I will, but where will I get information from?"

"They like you; they're always saying nice things about you," Camilla said.

After chatting a while longer, they paid their tabs and left. Driving back to the office, Lynette and Camilla continued their conversation about aging program issues while Angela listened quietly.

Chapter – Six

AGING PROGRAM PROBLEMS

Many of the senior workers were assigned to the county aging programs for job training. This resulted in Angela frequently monitoring the training the workers were receiving. During her visits, Velma, the Woodrow County Coordinator, and Cheryl, the Scott County Coordinator were always asking her questions about the Jefferson County Program. Sometimes, Cheryl would ask more detailed questions as if she was preparing a paper. During Angela's conversations with Cheryl or Velma, they often shared information with her about things they heard. When Angela asked where they had gotten their information, they always told her that Susan, Camilla, or Lynette had told them. Listening to them, Angela realized they were being told a great deal of misleading information that was keeping them stirred up with the idea of pulling from under the Commission.

Cheryl and Velma had been led to believe that Ms. Henderson was in charge of the county senior centers. However, they were both mistaken. The governing officials of the small towns took responsibility for the centers and the center managers. Those town officials paid all the expenses and salaries of the center managers.

During Angela's conversations with the two county coordinators, she got the impression that they were trying to confirm the information they were getting from Camilla and Lynette. After Angela became aware of what they were trying to do, she decided to stop answering their questions. It was not that, the other three county coordinators didn't ask questions; their questions were more in line with learning how they could improve the services they were providing. During Angela's visits to those counties, the coordinators would ask her to share information about the Jefferson County program they could benefit from.

When Clara, the Clair County Aging Program Coordinator, asked Angela for information, Angela took the time to explain the setup. During one of Angela's visits to Clair County, Clara took out her contract with Susan to show Angela. As Angela read the sections highlighted and listened to Clara talk, she could see that the wording allowed the county coordinators to operate more independently. It was a well-written contract, but the county coordinators' beliefs of how they were to function were misunderstood based on how Camilla and Lynette treated them. It was easy for Angela to understand because Camilla and Lynette treated the county aging program staff as if they were employees of the Area Agency on Aging. On several occasions, Angela had heard Camilla and Lynette chastising the county program staff. It was clear to Angela that neither Camilla nor Lynette understood how to work with contractors and their employees effectively. How they treated county program employees led Cheryl and Velma to believe they should have the same rights and benefits the Commission staff received. When the Commission staff received salary increases, Cheryl and Velma expected Susan to put more money into their budgets so they could give their staff increases.

Four of the five county aging programs were set up under the management of a non-profit organization that had been specifically established to serve as contract overseers. The fifth county aging program came under the management of the county commissioner in the county it was located in. Even though their board chairman signed the contract, two of the county program coordinators seem not to understand their relationship with the Commission.

Even though Angela was aware that the county coordinators were not pleased with how Camilla and Lynette treated their staff, Angela refused to comment because she did not want to be accused of getting involved when it was not her program.

As time passed, hardly a week passed without someone telling Angela about the aging program and their problems. Angela attended all of the aging program meetings. She would brief them on how well their programs worked together, and she would learn more about what they were doing—hearing all the information enabled Angela to see the pros and cons of operating the aging program.

One afternoon while Angela was in the conference room preparing a glass of iced tea, Jerry, one of the division directors, came in. While waiting for the coffee to perk, Jerry started talking about Scott County pulling away. He told Angela that the subject always came up when the aging program had shortfalls in it's' budget that could not be accounted for. Jerry then asked Angela if she was in the office when Susan and David had a heated argument about her budget shortfalls. He said Mr. Percy dared not confront Susan about her overspending problems, but David constantly questioned her. Angela told Jerry that being in the field most of the time, she missed out on things going on in the office. Jerry then started talking about the pull-out efforts that were being whispered about. He said that he believed Susan was behind the plot to pull the aging program from under the Commission. Angela acknowledged that she, too, was hearing rumors. She told him that she could sense something was up because Cheryl, the Scott County Program Coordinator, would ask her detailed questions about the Jefferson County Program. She told Jerry that the subject would always come up like a hot news break.

"Well…," Jerry said. *"Just keep your ears open, and you'll hear a lot of stuff."*

Angela started smiling. *"Jerry, people are always whispering, telling me things to be watchful of."*

Jerry then told Angela that Mr. Percy refused to believe that the aging program could be taken and that Mr. Percy thinks the executive committee has the power to prevent it.

"That committee is made up of both Republicans and Democrats, you can never say what they will or will not do," Angela said.

"You're right. Have you been paying attention to the fighting between our county and state political contenders?" Jerry commented.

"Horrible, isn't it? Can you believe educated, men can carry on like that?" Angela said.

"Who do you think will win in Scott and Clair County?" Jerry asked.

"Who knows? Only time will tell."

"Blair and I have been talking," Jerry said, *"We believe things could change if Republicans get into power."*

"I doubt if we will change," Angela said. *"We've always been a democratic state."*

Weeks later at the aging program quarterly meetings, the guest speaker from the US Census Bureau provided information about the regional censuses and how the census report affected federal funding allocations. Because of its growth, Scott County was used as an example. The speaker pointed out that the population numbers showed that Scott County was rapidly growing, but their growth was with the younger, wealthier population and not its' older poverty-stricken citizens. He explained that the county would be less likely to receive increases in federal funds to support the older poverty-stricken citizens, mainly because they had so few. After the presentation, the speaker allowed the group to ask questions, and Angela noticed that Cheryl was the most vocal of the county coordinators. She went so far as to say that Scott County was going after every dollar they thought was available to them. The speaker then highly praised her and suggested that the other county coordinators take the same approach. Considering no one else had a question or comment, the speaker concluded his presentation.

The group then took a break. During the break, Cheryl bragged about the compliments she had been given. Unfortunately, she didn't realize that the other county coordinators were not impressed. After

Cheryl had walked away, Angela overheard a conversation between three coordinators. They were saying that Cheryl seemed not to have understood that the county's growth in wealth would hinder them from getting more federal money for the poor elderly because there were so few. Realizing that Angela was standing nearby and may have heard their conversation, they changed the subject.

Later that evening, after the close of business, Clara called Angela at home for a chat. In a roundabout way, she wanted to know if Scott County could get more money if their county's aging population was not growing. Angela reiterated some of the things the speaker had told them.

"Yes," Clara said. *"But Cheryl is telling people that Scott County will get all this money."*

"Perhaps they will," Angela said. *"There are other types of grants she can apply for."*

Angela's statement got Clara's attention. It was apparent from the excitement in her voice tone when she asked; *"What kind of grants?"*

Angela told Clara about the various types of funds and how one would apply for the money. She explained that to get grant money, you would have to conduct research and carry out surveys to substantiate your eligibility and needs.

"Are you saying that Cheryl will go through the trouble of conducting research and applying for grants?"

"I don't know," Angela said.

"Well, if she does, believe it or not, we'll hear about it."

"Perhaps you will."

"By the way, I know you heard what we were talking about during our break."

"Yes, I did."

"Well, any comments?"

"No."

Angela knew Clara was trying to get her to criticize Cheryl, but she wasn't going that far. Clara then told her that she had spoken to her program board chairman and one of the county commissioners, and they suggested she call Angela. She went on to tell Angela that her county commissioners spoke very highly of her.

"Thanks for telling me," Angela said.

As they continued talking about different things, Angela gave Clara information on what she needed to do to bring in more money for her program. From talking to Clara, Angela realized that Cheryl had each county coordinator confused. Cheryl spoke a great deal about the two AAA Directors who had pulled away from the Regional Planning Commissions/Council of Governments in their area and set up as independent stand-alone. The Dayton AAA Director traveled throughout the state, bragging about the money his programs were bringing in after coming from under the council of governments. Hearing all the bragging Cheryl believed she could do great things if Scott County also became independent. It was apparent she wanted very much to be a stand-alone. The things she talked about and the words that seemed to make an impression on her were independence and more money.

When the Dayton County AAA Director talked about the money, he failed to tell them that he was taking advantage of the free labor he was getting from the Senior Employment Program. He was wise enough to sign up for all the free help he could get; he served as a mentor, signing his program up as a training site for students.

Another essential point Cheryl was unable to understand was the Jefferson County programs came under the Jefferson County Commission, and the Commission had the money to support the program. Cheryl failed to recognize that Dayton and Jefferson County AAAs contracted with individual townships. Whereas the Commission AAA contracted with non-profit organizations in four of their five counties and the county commission in one. Unfortunately, the non-profits had no other types of funds other than the aging program money. The non-profit heads had little to nothing to do with managing the programs or the employees. They were elderly citizens sitting on boards. The county coordinators were the true overseers and managers of the aging programs and all of the aging program staff answered to them.

Chapter – Seven

SHOCKWAVE - NEW GOVERNOR

Angela was frequently pulled aside and given information about issues unrelated to her programs. In a conversation with two friends, Angela told them she was being bombarded with information that didn't concern her. She told them that hardly a week went by without someone calling her on the telephone or pulling her aside and providing her with the latest information. Her friends laughed, and then Deborah pointed out that all agencies and businesses have employees like that. They want you to think they know everything that goes on.

"We refer to those employees as busybodies. They always seem to have the latest news," Vanessa said.

"They remind me of news reporters," Deborah said. "They're always getting the top story."

The three then started laughing.

"Y'all are right, but I'm trying not to get involved," Angela said.

"Well, good luck," Deborah said with a chuckle.

"I wonder what would happen if Scott County was successful and pulled from under the Planning Commission," Deborah commented.

"According to what I've been reading, they will not be able to pull away."

"*Why not?*" Deborah asked.

"*Because of their population,*" Angela said. "*They're not large enough to stand alone.*"

Angela then proceeded to tell them about some of the federal and state guidelines she had been reading. She informed them that Scott County did not have the required population to become an Independent AAA. At that time, their population was around 43,600, with growth projections of 100 thousand by the end of the year 2000, and under federal guidelines, they needed a population of 100 thousand or more to be an Independent AAA.

"*Angela, you said that their population was rapidly growing. Maybe they'll try again.*" Vanessa said.

"*Perhaps they will.*" Angela agreed.

"*Girl…, you've been doing a lot of research,*" Deborah commented. "*How is it benefitting you?*"

"*I just like knowing all the facts.*"

"*Maybe they're the ones that need to do some research,*" Deborah said.

Several days later, while Angela was eating lunch in the conference room, Grace, the aging program secretary, joined her. While chatting about different things, Grace asked if she had heard about Susan's problems with the State Commission on Aging (COA). Angela, not being aware, allowed Grace to give her the details. Grace told her that Susan was facing a non-stop challenge by COA to get her to come back under the statewide meals program.

The five counties the Commission AAA served were unique among the state aging programs. The Commission AAA was the only one that contracted with county non-profit organizations, instead of individual townships. All of the aging services in those counties came under the non-profits. When Angela inquired why their agency was the only region in the state that did not fall under the statewide meals contract, Grace provided some background. She told Angela that federal dollars had been plentiful and easy to obtain during the earlier growth years of the program, and the aging programs had more money than they could spend. During those years, the Commission AAA took on the task of getting the counties to build their kitchens, purchase equipment, and hire staff to prepare daily meals. This change brought great benefits to the counties; it created jobs, and many businesses profited because most of the goods and products were purchased from county vendors. Grace went on to tell her that during earlier years, the state had contracted with various contractors who did not push to have statewide control of the meals program. But as time passed, contractors changed due to a state bidding law being put into effect. When Marco Meals, Inc. won the state bid, they had requested statewide control for the meals program, but the Planning Commission was unwilling to give up their kitchens and return to the meals being brought in. During that period, Marco Meals, Inc. representatives tried to persuade the Planning Commission to come under the statewide meals contract. However, after realizing they were not making any progress, Marco Meals, Inc. management changed their tactics and put the responsibility of getting the Commission to join in the hands of COA. When the COA began pressuring the Commission, they quickly learned that the Commission would not give in. The Commission's unwillingness to give in created a constant battle that was written up in newspapers around the state. To aid the Commission in their fight, the senior citizens they served spoke out by writing and calling their county commissioners, state senators, representatives, and the state Commission on Aging.

The seniors in the counties loved the meals prepared in their county kitchens. They had input on the foods served and did not want to return to the contract meals. Listening to Grace, Angela better understood the problems Susan had to deal with. She realized that being the AAA Director did not come without opposition.

It seemed like problems were always coming up, either in-house or in the field. The aging program had lost its position to serve Jefferson County years earlier, and there were never-ending rumors that Scott County was trying to pull away. However, despite the troublesome things she had to deal with, it appeared that Susan did not allow them to take away her joy of living.

Many people around the state saw Susan as a party woman who loved celebrating. There was hardly a week that went by without Susan finding something to celebrate. The aging program staff meetings were held outside of the office where attendees could order a cocktail if they wished. Knowing this, everyone invited always attended.

That year, as the Christmas Holiday season was approaching, most people were talking about things they would do with their families. Whereas Susan was busy planning her New Year's Eve Party. The people who were fortunate to get invited looked forward to the occasion. For her home gatherings, she was very selective, inviting only a few Commission staff members; Angela was one of the few she invited. The aging in-house staff consisted of more than fifteen employees, but Susan only included one of them in her personal social life, and that was Lynette. Among the many guests invited to her parties was Jeffery, the Deputy Director of the State Commission on Aging. On the evening of the New Year's Eve Party, Jeffery kept everyone laughing. He talked about Alabama Politics and the characters running for various offices. The politicians who wanted to get ahead had already started campaigning. Posters were everywhere. Despite the fact Jeffery was not running for public office, he managed to carry around a stack of campaign posters during the campaign season. It was said that when he saw a campaign poster he could joke about, he would stop along the road and take one of the posters. On the evening of the get-together, he had brought in a selection of posters. When he started showing the posters and making comments, the guests roared with laughter. He then got other guests to participate by mimicking what they thought the candidates may have been thinking when taking the pictures. The guests' impromptu speeches began to sound like a comedian in a comedy club. The guests' jokes about the politicians kept the crowd roaring throughout the night.

After spending hours listening to Jeffery's jokes, Angela could see why Susan would always invite him. He was a delightful party guest and was known for being a person who could express himself in a manner that captured your attention.

He was a tall lanky fella with features similar to those of a basketball player, he was often asked what team he had played on in college. He was a well-groomed brunette with a neatly trimmed mustache and beard.

During the spring of, all the people running for various public offices were campaigning in full force; posters were everywhere. The median along the interstates and other roadways was cluttered with campaign posters. You couldn't find one telephone or light pole that didn't have five or more campaign posters attached. The trees and median along the highways were covered with posters. The discussion on all the radio stations was complaints from citizens who resented the trashy effects created by the thousands of posters and the uncalled-for statements made by candidates about other candidates.

The Commission division directors were very concerned about the six counties the Commission served. Each time they went out in the counties, they brought back campaign posters of all the candidates running for office. Around the office, they talked and laughed about what each candidate was saying about the other candidates. But none of the candidates could outdo the fights that were going on between Hudson and Commissioner Miller. They were competing for commissioner in Scott County. Their battles were fierce; Hudson, the Republican candidate, took the position that he was better experienced at making things happen. He would take on fights about everything that got the media's attention. The campaign had long lost its' substance of what competing candidates could do for the people; it had taken on the typical political fights, the Democrats against the Republicans. Hudson and Miller's competition was a bitter mudslinging, back-stabbing good old southern boy fight. It seemed like no other politicians could fight like Scott County Republicans. Together with two other young radical Republican candidates running for office, Hudson felt they could move the small rural county forward. The county residents often referred to the three candidates as members of the 'I want it now generation.' The three candidates preached disassociating themselves from the district and establishing their regional planning commission.

Jefferson County also had its' dirty politics going on. However, most of the citizens talked about the fights going on for the state governor's position. Among the many candidates running for state governor were two well-known Democrats; the battles between the two were fierce. They fought hard to get the nomination, but the votes in the June primary

picture, with the two facing each other in a runoff. The
ative candidate won by a few thousand votes. However,
refused to accept the polls' results. He claimed the other
olated primary regulations by encouraging Republicans to
cross over and vote as Democrats.

During that time, Alabama was an open primary state, and it was perfectly legal to vote your choice. Whereas today, when voting in the primary election, one must choose to vote for either Democrats or Republicans, and a voter is then issued the proper ballot.

Unfortunately, the fighting between the two candidates running for state governor did not cease, and their dispute made its way to the State Supreme Court. The Court told the Democrats to declare one of the two as the winner by default or hold another primary. The party then picked their choice, but the fight didn't end. Alabamians, being accustomed to a one-party state where anybody could vote in the primary, were outraged. Outraged, Alabamians took their frustration to the polls in November and voted for a relatively unknown Republican candidate. When the final votes were counted, the Republican candidate had won the election with 56 percent of the voters. The numbers resulted in him receiving the most votes ever for a gubernatorial candidate. His election surprised Alabamians because the last Republican Governor had left office 113 years earlier at the end of reconstruction.

When Angela got to work the morning after the election, several staff members were standing in the reception area reading the newspapers and talking.

Belinda laughingly said to Angela, *"You look beat."*

"What did you do all night?" Valeria asked Angela.

"I was up all night watching the numbers come in. Will someone please tell me who in the hell is Hanson?" Angela asked with laughter.

They all started laughing.

"I don't know," Valeria said. *"Other than, he's our new Governor, and he is a Republican."*

"Yes, and we'll soon find out what he's about," Shelley commented as they left the reception area and headed to their offices.

Chapter – Eight

COA NEW DEPUTY DIRECTOR

Throughout the day, staff members gathered to discuss the election's outcome and the newly elected governor. As time passed, discussions in the office and around the state began to focus on the unknowns being appointed to serve as cabinet heads.

The Commission had most of its programs coming under various state departments. As a result, the Commissioner Division Directors were more concerned about the cabinets their programs came under.

Most people in the aging network were hoping that the existing state aging commissioner would be re-appointed. Although a few had major problems with the state commissioner, they were still rallying behind him. To gain full support for the current commissioner, the Council of Governments Executive Directors held meetings to discuss means of publicly promoting him. In a meeting held in the Commission conference room, the Council of Governments (COG) Executives Directors, expressed their thoughts about the state commissioner. As Angela walked past the conference room door, which had been left slightly open, she overheard one of the COG Executives make the statement: *"I think it's better to keep the bastard, you know, instead of going out and hiring a bastard you don't know shit about."*

Angela thought the statement was hilarious, but she didn't laugh because she was concerned about being heard. Though she had only been in the aging network a few years, she had gotten to know the state commissioner quite well. Her relationship with the state commissioner had grown because of his relationship with Mr. Mason, the SEP National Representative. The two men were close friends who had known each other for many years. Mr. Mason had told Angela that the state commissioner was an uncompromising man who didn't take a lot of crap from anyone. Understanding the close professional relationship the two men shared, Angela hoped the commissioner would be re-appointed.

While most people in the aging network talked about the commissioner's position, very few were concerned about the deputy director's position. Mainly because they viewed the deputy director as a person they would not have to contend with. COA's current deputy director was a nice guy who was appreciated and well-liked. Angela had gotten to know and like him at Susan's New Year's Eve party.

While the Planning Commission staff were focused on who would become the next Commissioner, of the State Commission on Aging (SCOA), none of them noticed the excitement being displayed by Camilla and Lynette. Susan had told the two that the incoming governor was appointing her as deputy director of the Commission on Aging. Their excitement was based on Susan's leaving would open the door for upward mobility for the two of them.

During the last week of December and the first week in January, the newly elected governor had speeded up announcing his cabinet appointees. For the State Commission on Aging, the governor chose a well-educated Black man to serve as Executive Director. To the surprise of everyone in the aging network, Susan was appointed COA Deputy Director. Her appointment was a big surprise, for she was known throughout the network as a person who loved to party. On the other hand, the executive director was unknown to people in the network. Many people in the aging network saw the two appointees as a joke, especially after the former commissioner had run the department for over twenty years.

When the information about Susan's appointment became widely known, people who knew of the problems the Commission had with the state agency regarding the meals program believed that this was a blessing for the Commission. However, those who truly knew Susan were aware of her resentment of the in-direct cost the Commission charged the programs that came under its umbrella.

Susan's thinking was in line with many AAA Directors across the United States. Many of them expressed that it would be better for the AAAs if they came from under the councils of governments. Susan's beliefs were based mainly on the two AAA Directors who had pulled from the councils of governments years earlier. The two AAA Directors talked a lot about their independence and total control over the money they received.

Three days before Susan was scheduled to take her new job, she came in late one morning and turned in her resignation letter. The following day she joined the staff for a going away party at one of her favorite restaurants. Immediately following the celebration, Camilla and Lynette left with Susan but did not return to the office.

With Susan now gone, the Commission Personnel Committee appointed Camilla as interim AAA Director, and Lynette was moved upward into Camilla's former position. However, these appointments were temporary while the personnel committee searched for a new AAA Director. The personnel committee immediately put 'help wanted' ads in local and national newsletters and newspapers. When the resumes started coming in, the secretaries thought nothing of the large number of applications, mainly because they all believed that the job would be given to Camilla, and the advertisement was simply a matter of policy.

Camilla had worked with Susan and the previous AAA Directors for more than fifteen years. It was assumed that she was the most qualified candidate for the job. Lynette was also expected to be promoted to fill Camilla's former position. To ensure that the appointment and the promotion were made, Susan got the help of Commissioner Rucker to support the two applicants. They wrote letters to the Commission Personnel Committee, strongly advocating the appointment of Camilla and the promotion of Lynette. To gain regional and state support for her recommendations, Susan contacted the other COG Directors, city mayors, and county commissioners asking them to support her choices.

Unfortunately, Susan was unaware that neither Camilla nor Lynette was considered suitable for the top position. They had created enemies in three counties by chastising the county coordinators and county program staff. Susan was also unaware that the county coordinators were hoping that neither of the two was appointed to fill her former job. As time passed, Susan began to hear rumors about the negative feelings some had about Camilla. With this knowledge regarding Camilla's standing for the job and Susan's resentment of the Commission's in-direct rate, Susan was now faced with a challenge she had not expected. She now had to devise another plan to gain the support of county leaders who were not leaning in the direction she was hoping for.

In light of the fact several Scott County officials had previously made attempts to take the aging program, Susan was confident, that if she could get their support she could get Camilla appointed AAA. With this idea, she went to the newly elected Republican County Commissioners and negotiated with them. Their job was to go to the Republican County Commissioners in the other four counties and try to gain their support. She guaranteed them that if they could get Camilla appointed, it would be easy to take the aging program from the Commission. Even though she had previously been AAA Director for years, she had never researched the requirements for taking the aging program from an existing overseer. Nor was she aware of the many obstacles she would have to face. She was operating under the assumption that all they needed to do was present the Commission Executive Committee with resolutions stating that they would be pulling away. She had never considered that each county would have to agree to pull away. At that time, some of the officials in Scott County were the only ones excited about making a move. Unknowingly, they could not pull away by themselves. There were other factors Susan would later learn that would hinder her conquest.

However, she never took the time to research and evaluate the outcome of taking the program.

In her effort to gain support, she would travel around the region throughout the week, lobbying to ensure Camilla would be the next AAA Director. Her determination was so strong she went outside of the six-county region to promote Camilla. Although her scheme appeared persuasive to some, a few individuals sent their applications in.

During the first week of March, the State Gerontological Society (SGS) was holding its annual conference in Mobile, AL. Everyone in the aging network was planning to attend. Attendees would be saying goodbye to their long-time Aging State Commissioner and welcoming the incoming Commissioner.

The Commission staff attending the conference signed out company vehicles for the trip, but Angela drove her automobile because of her plans after the conference. Angela and her daughter were planning a shopping trip to Foley, AL, and spending a couple of days at Perdido Beach. Angela and her daughter Keshia arrived at the hotel ahead of the other staff. After unpacking, they left the hotel and went out to get something to eat.

Later that evening, Angela went downstairs and joined her colleagues. While waiting for the opening reception to start, they went into the cocktail lounge, ordered drinks, and sat around chatting about the newly elected governor, his cabinet appointees, and their trip to Mobile. Judy, the Commission's accountant, began telling Angela about their trip. She told Angela that she and three other staff members had traveled to Mobile with Lynette, who was driving one of the Commission SUVs. Listening while Judy gave the details, Belinda suddenly interrupted and started talking about Lynette's driving. She had learned firsthand that Lynette had a bad habit of pissing other drivers off. She said that it was frightening riding in the vehicle with Lynette behind the wheel. She explained that Lynette had pulled over in front of another vehicle, and the driver had started honking his horn. Lynette then started honking her horn and giving the drivers the finger. The other co-workers who were in the SUV began laughing because they were aware of Lynette's bad driving habits. Everyone in the agency knew that Lynette was known for speeding and yelling out the window telling other drivers to get the hell off the road if they couldn't drive.

Though the usage of the phrase *road rage* was not commonly used in those days, Lynette's behavior would have been classified as extreme road rage. Staff members who had the unfortunate experience of riding with Lynette talked about her driving and the number of speeding tickets she had gotten. Listening to Belinda's talk, it was evident that she did not wish to travel back with Lynette.

"Sounds like this was your first time riding with Lynette," Angela said with a giggle.

"Yes, and I'll never get in another vehicle if she's driving."

Shelley interrupted Belinda and asked if she had made plans on how she would get back to Birmingham.

"I'll ride back with Angela," Belinda told her.

Angela then told them that she wasn't planning to go straight back because she and Keshia had made plans to do some shopping and spend some time in Perdido Beach. Belinda then started negotiating with Angela trying to get her to put off her shopping for another time. The other girls began teasing Belinda, telling her that they were all taking a chance riding with Lynette and she would be going back with them.

After they had finished joking around, their conversation shifted to the election outcome when a couple of Angela's colleagues from another region joined them. Being inquisitive, Carol from Mobile asked which one of them had voted for Hanson.

"Not me," Shelley firmly stated.

"Neither did I," Valeria from Camden commented.

"And neither did I," Belinda said.

At that moment, Carol questioned the others, asking them if either of them had voted for the new governor. When they asked Angela, Angela tried to brush it off by telling them that one's voting choice was personal. Remembering that Angela had come to work the day after the election and asked if they had voted for the new governor, Belinda reminded her that she had told them she had voted for him. At that point,

Angela acknowledged that she had indeed voted for the Republican candidate, but she never anticipated he would win.

"Nobody I have spoken to seems to know anything about him," Valeria said.

After Valeria's statement, several others started questioning Angela, asking why she had voted for Hanson.

"Am I on trial?" Angela jokingly asked.

"Girl, we just want to know what made you vote for an unknown Republican," Carol said.

Angela then proceeded to tell them that she had reached her tolerance limit for the bickering of the two Democratic candidates. She went on to say she would have voted for Deputy Dog had the name been on the ballot. She told them she wasn't a party person, and she had always voted a split ticket because she had associates who were Democrats and some who were Republicans.

"Who are your associates?" Carol asked.

"I bet they're White," Valeria said.

"They are members of my military unit," Angela told them.

Angela went on to tell them that she had marched and protested during the mid-1960s for the right to vote her choice.

"You're lucky," Carol said. *"Many people I know would think you're nuts for voting for a Republican."*

"Yes, I know that," Angela said with a giggle.

"All of my family is like that," Judy said. *"We all vote for democrats."*

"Well... all I can say is, Hanson, had better be good," Valeria commented.

"I just hope he's better than the complainers on the democratic ticket," Angela said.

Angela told them she was fed up with the two fighting before the primary, and when they ended up in the state supreme court, they lost her vote.

Shelley then looked at her watch, and seeing the time, she suggested they start heading toward the ballroom. As they strolled along, talking, they could see the corridor which led to the ballroom was very crowded.

"I don't like being in large crowds; why don't we wait a few minutes," Judy said.

A man passing by heard them talking and said, *"You'll probably be waiting a long time."*

"Why do you say that?" Valeria asked the man.

"People are going through a receiving line," he said.

Valeria then asked if either of them had seen Camilla or Lynette. A lady standing nearby heard Valeria and told them that Camilla and Lynette were standing in line with the new state commissioner and his deputy director.

"Hum, I wonder why," Belinda said.

Chapter – Nine

URGENT TELEPHONE CALL

A few minutes later, Valeria cheerfully said as they were walking toward the crowd. *"I see them now. Look at the big smile on Camilla's face."*

From a distance, one could see Camilla and Lynette's expressions. They were glowing with joy. Looking at them, one could have assumed they had been appointed to some state cabinet-level position. As the line moved forward, they continued chatting. Valeria turned to the group and suggested they all embrace Susan when they approached her.

"I'm not going to hug that woman; she doesn't like me," Judy said.

Judy then whispered to Angela, suggesting they get out of the line to talk. As the two walked away from the crowd, different people approached them, asking about the AAA job position. Several stated that they had submitted job applications, even after being told that Camilla would most likely get the appointment.

"What do you say when people ask about the AAA position?" Judy asked.

"I tell them I don't know."

They both agreed that most of the Commission staff believed Camilla would get the appointment.

"I hope she doesn't spend money as Susan did…. To be honest, I'm praying that she doesn't get the job," Judy said.

Angela was taken by surprise upon hearing Judy make that statement. *"Are you serious?"* Angela asked.

"I'm dead serious."

"Are you going to tell me why?" Angela asked.

At that moment, John, one of Camilla's counterparts from another region, walked up.

"I'll tell you later," Judy whispered.

"I believe you two beautiful ladies are going in the wrong direction," John said.

John then reached and hugged Judy, then turned and embraced Angela.

"I can tell you're trying to flatter us," Judy said.

"No, just stating a fact," he said with a big smile.

John was a nice-looking medium-built, light brown complexion man in his early 40s. He stood approximately 6'2" tall, with his weight in proportion to his height. He wore his thick bushy black hair nicely cut and neatly trimmed. On that day, he wore a brown three-piece suit with a tie that matched the stripes on his shirt. John was a friendly guy known by everyone in the aging network. However, he was not known to be a man who spent much time talking about politics, but on that day, he was very talkative. He immediately started talking about the election outcome. Angela was somewhat surprised, for she had known him for several years but had never heard him speak so candidly about an issue. Hearing the things he said, it was apparent that he was pleased to see a Black man appointed to head up a state cabinet.

Considering John was now with them, Judy could not continue the conversation she had pulled Angela from the line to talk about. After the three had chatted for a while about the incoming and outgoing state commissioners, they noticed the line had gotten shorter, so they decided to make their way back over to the area.

"Angela, you're not saying much," John commented.

"What would you like for me to say?"

John smiled but didn't say anything else on the subject of race. He knew Angela was the equal employment opportunity non-commission advisor (EEO-NCO) for her military unit, and she took her job seriously.

Judy whispered as the line moved forward, telling Angela that she thought it was inappropriate for Camilla and Lynette to be standing in the receiving line. Angela smiled but did not respond, considering John was still with them.

Shortly afterward, they were approaching the receiving line. John approached Commissioner Rucker and then Susan shaking their hands and congratulating them. He then shook hands with Camilla and Lynette and congratulated them, considering he had heard the rumors about their upcoming promotions. As John moved forward, Judy and Angela followed, shaking hands and making comments.

"So…, you're Ms. Marshall. It's a pleasure to meet you," Commissioner Rucker said with a smile.

"The pleasure is mine, and I'm looking forward to working with you."

"I'm looking forward to working with you also." He said in a flattering tone as he was still holding her hand.

"I believe you'll like being in the aging network," Angela told him.

"So far, so good," he commented.

Angela then told him that she would be calling to make an appointment to come to see him when the Senior Employment Program Representative came to town. She then moved on, congratulating and expressing kind words to Susan. After which, she greeted Camilla and Lynette with a handshake.

A short time later, Angela and Judy were seated in an area away from the crowd, talking.

"Staff members believe our problems are over now that Susan is at the State Commission," Judy said.

"Well.., I can't comment because I don't know," Angela stated.

"Watch and see what happens. I think Susan will do everything she can to hurt Mr. Percy."

"How can she hurt him?" Angela asked.

Judy told Angela that she was certain that Susan would try to pull the aging program from under the Commission and set it up in Scott County. She went on to say that Susan had always complained about the in-direct rate.

Angela chuckled; *"she's not the only one complaining, but how can he lower the rate?"*

"By reducing some of the overhead expense," Judy said.

"Then, maybe he should."

"Watch and see; our problems are just getting started," Judy said.

Judy then inquired about what Angela and Susan talked about when they were together. Angela told her that Susan believed the in-direct cost was too heavily imposed on the aging program. Judy laughed, then told Angela that Susan probably said the in-cost rate caused her overspending.

"She did," Angela smiled and said.

"Susan attributes all of her financial shortfalls to the in-direct cost, but it's her overspending habits that cause the problems," Judy said.

She then went on to tell Angela that Mr. Percy had to take money out of the Commission reserve funds three consecutive years to bail the aging program out. She went on to say, that had Susan managed the aging money better, she would never have gone into overspending. She said they had spent all morning, one Saturday looking for $85K in the aging program budget.

"What was the problem?" Angela asked.

Judy said that Susan was planning to attend some conferences, but when she turned in her request for advance money, she was unable to issue the checks, because the money wasn't in the aging program budget.

Angela started laughing; *"Now... I understand why the two of you don't like each other."*

Judy continued, stating that she had told Mr. Percy several months earlier that the Commission would have to use Commission reserves to cover the aging program shortfalls for the current year.

"How did you come to that conclusion?"

"Because Susan's spending has already exceeded the projected quarterly expenditures."

"Oh well," Angela said.

Judy said that she believed that Susan would try to take the aging program because of her lack of understanding about in-direct costs.

"Do you honestly believe that?"

"Yes, I have told Mr. Percy what I'm telling you."

"What does he say?"

"The same old thing… We'll have to wait and see."

"By the way, did y'all ever find the $85K?"

"Hell no! But that wasn't the worst part about it. While we were working, Susan was busy planning her trip."

"Now, how do you know that?"

Judy told Angela that it was obvious from the stack of pictures of hotels Susan was looking at. Judy went on to say that she wished she could take trips like that on Commission funds.

"Oh well," Angela responded with a giggle.

Angela knew what Judy was talking about because each time she and Susan had talked, Susan was always telling her about trips she had gone on.

After talking for a while longer, they decided to go back toward the ballroom. As they walked down the long corridor, they saw several co-workers coming toward them. As they met and started talking, one of the co-workers interrupted and told Angela that she had been paged.

Shortly afterward the hotel paging system came back on, paging Angela for an urgent telephone call. Being somewhat surprised by the word urgent, Angela immediately excused herself and rushed over to a house telephone and called her room to check on Keshia. After learning that Keshia was okay, Angela went to the front desk.

Not knowing who was calling, thoughts were racing through Angela's mind as the hotel desk clerk escorted her down the corridor to an office where she was to take the call. When they entered, the desk clerk picked up the telephone and announced that Angela was present.

She then gave Angela the telephone and walked out, closing the door
behind her.

"Hello, this is Angela."

"Ms. Marshall, this is Chairman Robertson."

Surprised to hear his voice, she said: *"Yes, sir."*

*"We have gone through all the resumes for the AAA position and dis-
covered yours' is not in the pile."*

For a brief moment, Angela was silent, not knowing how to respond.

"Are you there? Did you hear what I said?"

"Yes, sir, I did."

"Why didn't you submit your resume?"

"I didn't know the job was open to the general public."

"What gave you that idea?"

"I was told that the job would be given to Camilla."

*"Hum… is that so? Well, the deadline for the resumes is 4:45 p.m.
Friday. We want your application in before 4:30 p.m. Can we depend
on you?"*

"Yes, sir."

After terminating the call, Angela was speechless. She didn't know
how to react or what to say. She knew that people who knew her would
inquire about the urgent telephone call. To regain her composure, she
went back to her hotel room to tell Keshia about the call. She told
Keshia that something had come up that required her attention back
in Birmingham, and they would be leaving early Friday morning. Of
course, Keshia was disappointed, for she had been looking forward to the
shopping trip and the time they would be spending on the beach. After
sharing as much information as necessary, Angela went back downstairs
and joined her colleagues.

Just as she had thought, people who knew her started asking about
the nature of the urgent telephone call. She told them a lie, stating that
her daughter needed to talk to her. Still surprised and uneasy about the
telephone call, Angela excused herself from the presence of the people
she knew well.

As the opening of the general session drew near, the attendees started going into the auditorium. The platform had all the familiar faces, with Commissioner Rucker being the only new face among them. As various speakers got up and made their remarks, the more than 1400 attendees sat waiting to hear the comments the outgoing state commissioners would make.

Finally, the former state commissioner approached the podium to bid farewell.

Commissioner Jemison was a tall heavyset White man in his late 60's. From being in his presence when he and Mr. Mason were talking, Angela knew that he was hoping to be reappointed to serve under the new governor.

When he started speaking, the crowd was quiet, but the silence quickly changed to laughter when he began to joke.

"Let me see the hands of those staying here at the Stouffer."

As hands went up, the Commissioner commented: *"Great, isn't it? My only problem was, I had to buy some cheap luggage to take these plush towels and bathrobes home."*

At that moment, some of the people in the auditorium started snickering.

"He sounds serious." A voice in the crowd said.

"Damn right! I am serious." He responded without cracking a smile. *"The Commission on Aging is paying a helluva lot of money for these rooms."* He chuckled then added; *"but that's now Commissioner Rucker's problem."*

After a few other statements that brought on laughter, the former Commissioner concluded his remarks and left the platform.

The Master of Ceremony (MC) then introduced the newly appointed Commissioner, Dr. Rucker. He stated that he and Dr. Rucker had spoken on the telephone several times, and Commissioner Rucker had cautioned him about the correct spelling of his name. It was obvious, people in the audience thought nothing of the statement, for there was not a whisper of any kind made. After he finished his remarks, Commissioner Rucker got up to speak. As he stood looking toward the exit, where the former Commissioner was still shaking hands, Commissioner Rucker said, *"I'm not going to attempt to try to outdo the comments made by my predecessor."*

Commissioner Rucker was a nice-looking, tall medium-brown, Black man with a charming smile and deep dimples. He stood approximately 5'10" with his weight in proportion to his height. He was well-educated, with an impressive vocabulary. Dr. Rucker had come to the position after serving as a healthcare administrator in Los Angeles.

As he looked out over the crowd, he asked everyone to take out a pen and a piece of paper. He then proceeded to spell his name, clearly articulating each letter. After he finished, he asked if everyone had written the letters correctly. When the crowd responded appropriately, he stated that he wanted to make sure no one wrote him a letter using an F instead of an R. Those who were quick and replaced the R with an F snickered, releasing the tension many were feeling. The crowd then began to laugh as others in the audience, who perhaps were not paying attention, grasped what the change of letters would have spelled. Finally, after the crowd had ceased laughing, Commissioner Rucker proceeded with his remarks.

Chapter – Ten

AAA APPOINTMENT

After the gathering had ended, small groups stood around talking about things they had heard about him. During his speech, he expressed that he was a trusting man. Many said his trusting nature would get him in trouble, believing he could trust his cabinet colleagues. The general opinion of many Angela spoke with was he was by no means a politician. After talking with her colleagues a while longer, Angela returned to her room.

With all the activities going on, the next three days went by quickly. Finally, on Friday morning, Angela packed and loaded her car, and then joined her colleagues for breakfast. She informed them that something important had come up that required her attention back in Birmingham. Of course, several of her friends wanted to know why she couldn't deal with the issue the following Monday. Knowing she could not discuss the matter with anyone, Angela allowed her colleagues to assume she was returning home early to prepare for weekend military duty.

Five hours later, Angela was back in Birmingham. After dropping Keshia off at home, Angela went to the office, updated her resume, and gave it to Mr. Percy's secretary. Angela stood in the secretary's office watching as the secretary stamped the resume with the time. The secretary then picked up the telephone and called Commissioner Robertson and notified him that Angela's resume was in. Due to the aging staff being in Mobile, Angela knew that her resume for the AAA Director's position would not be known until the personnel committee started interviewing.

Two weeks later, Mr. Mason was in town to monitor the Senior Employment Program. As planned, he and Angela drove to Montgomery to visit Commissioner Rucker. As they traveled, they laughed and joked about Alabama Politics and the recent election outcome. Mr. Mason then congratulated Angela on getting her resume in for the AAA position. He flattered her, telling her that the national office would be losing a great director. He went on to tell her about the conference call they had gotten from three Commission Executive Committee members.

"You know that Camilla thinks she'll get that job," Angela said.

"Yes, they told us that Susan's former assistant was favored by several executive committee members, *"but they assured us that you would be selected as the next AAA Director."*

He went on to say that several national office staff members had sent letters praising her outstanding performance. Hearing Mr. Mason make those statements was gratifying to Angela. She believed that God was now using staff members of the national office to move her forward, promoting her to a higher level. Mr. Mason then pulled the letters from his jacket pocket and gave them to her to read. As Angela read each letter, she was overwhelmed by what they had said about her character and job performance. She didn't realize that the national staff thought so highly of her. Seeing the look on her face, Mr. Mason said, *"Of course, you know we give all of the directors' certificates of excellence and outstanding overall performance awards."*

Angela smiled because she knew he was joking. All of the project directors did not achieve their goals, whereas many far exceeded theirs. There were six letters, one from the executive director, two from regional representatives, two from financial auditors, and one from Mr. Mason.

After Angela and Mr. Mason had chatted a while longer about the

AAA job, Mr. Mason again started talking about the recent election. He wanted to hear what Angela's opinion was concerning the new governor. Angela told him that she had not formed an opinion. He told her he had spoken to many people around the state, and they had already formed an opinion and that their views were not very flattering.

"I have been told that the governor has appointed many of his cronies."

Angela giggled, *"I thought they all did that."*

"Well, I suppose they do. That's life everywhere you go, but I wonder how well he knew her."

"If not, he'll soon find out. You know, they are both from the same county." Angela said.

"No, I didn't know that. Is she a Republican?"

"I don't think so."

"Oh well, Alabama now has a Republican governor, and it appears he is surrounding himself with other Republicans."

"Isn't that the way it's supposed to be? You've heard the old saying, 'You scratch my back, and I'll scratch yours.'" Angela said with a chuckle.

Mr. Mason then started talking about other cabinet appointees. He mentions that many of the executives around the state believed that the governor had been pressured to get people appointed. He said many of the people he spoke to thought Commissioner Rucker did not possess the political savvy to run the department. With a chuckle, he went on to say that the governor had appointed some interesting characters to fill other cabinet positions. Angela acknowledged that she had also heard other people making unflattering statements about the various appointments the governor had made.

Mr. Mason then started talking about the state slots. The significance of his statement was a bit unclear, for Angela was unaware that the state had slots. He told her that the national office wanted to know if Commissioner Rucker was planning to allow the national office to continue managing the slots. As Angela listened she tried to comprehend what he was referring to.

"I'm confused," she said. *What do you mean about state slots?*

"Several national programs operate in the state," he said.

"I didn't know that," Angela responded.

"I'll have to explain it to Commissioner Rucker, then you'll understand."

A short time later, they were pulling into a parking space at the State Commission on Aging. Moments later, they were in Commissioner Rucker's office talking. After the two men had chatted awhile, getting to know each other, Mr. Mason commenced explaining the partnership the national office had enjoyed with the former state commissioner. In light of the fact Commissioner Rucker was new in his job, Mr. Mason took the opportunity to give him some background information. He then asked Commissioner Rucker if the national office could depend on retaining the partnership with him. Commissioner Rucker assured Mr. Mason that he saw no reason for that relationship to change. As Angela listened, she was able to obtain a greater understanding of the nature of the partnership. She learned that the Administration on Aging had awarded slots to states and national agencies, but Alabama had allowed two national agencies to administer their slots. She further got a clearer understanding of the state slots and the counties they were located in. Angela also learned that most of the state slots had been given to rural counties that had a high population of Black residents.

After concluding the business discussion, the two men began talking about other issues and getting to know each other better. At that moment, Angela decided to leave and go talk with several COA staff members. Approximately thirty minutes later, Angela returned. Mr. Mason then thanked Commissioner Rucker as he was getting up to leave.

"No," Commissioner Rucker said, *"I thought maybe the three of us would have lunch together."*

A week later, the Commission Personnel Committee started making arrangements to interview for the AAA position. During that time, the Commission staff became aware of the five in-house applicants who had been selected for interviews. Among the names were Angela's. Seeing that she had applied for the position, several staff members whispered, saying she was trying to climb the ladder too fast. Their statement was based on the fact that Angela had been with the Commission only twenty months, whereas the other applicants had been with the Commission for years. Staff members also whispered, saying that Angela and the other in-house staff were setting themselves up for a big disappointment because Camilla would most likely get the appointment. They were basing their statement on the fact that Camilla was thought to be the most qualified in light of the number of years she had served in her position.

One afternoon while Camilla and Angela were in the restroom touching up their make-up, Camilla turned to Angela and commented: *"Girl, I was surprised to learn you had submitted your resume for the job."*

Angela smiled, *"Yes I decided to take a chance."*

"Why didn't you tell me?" Camilla asked.

"I didn't think it was necessary," Angela said.

They continued chatting for a moment or two before leaving the restroom.

"Well, good luck," Camilla said with a smile as they headed back to their office.

"Thank you," Angela said, *"And the same to you."*

When the interviewing process started, Camilla was the eighth person they interviewed. After concluding her interview, she stunned the all-white male personnel committee with a bold warning. Camilla informed them that she would make sure the agency suffered if she didn't get the appointment. Committee members were stunned to have her threaten them, and after she had left the room, they sat back, talking and laughing about her comments.

The committee met three times weekly to interview applicants. After a couple of weeks had gone by and the committee had completed the interviewing process, they started deliberating. As the process went on, Angela's supporters never waived. As time passed, after each meeting, they would stop by her office and ask her how she was doing. Before leaving, they would always say *Simper fi (Semper Fidelis),* which means always faithful; the United States Marine Corps Motto.

As the days passed, whispering around the office continued. Several staff members strongly expressed their disappointment about Angela submitting her resume for the job. Hearing the comments, Angela began to feel disheartened. Knowing she was in the middle of a loyalty battle, she decided to withdraw her name. After getting home, she called the personnel committee chairman and informed him of her decision. He listened to all of her explanations but refused to accept her withdrawal. Later that evening, Angela received calls from several other personnel committee members. They each encouraged her to stay in the race and not make assumptions about how the results would pan out.

While the deliberation process was going on, Camilla was carrying out the duties of the AAA Director. It was apparent; that she felt confident she would be chosen. Staff members supporting her appointment had always said that Susan showed up, but Camilla did the work.

As nutrition services coordinator, Camilla was involved in all aspects of the daily meals program. She reviewed and approved the menus and forwarded them to Auburn University for certification. She monitored the county kitchens and performed food safety tests to ensure the meals prepared met health standards. She handled the contracts for the purchase of perishables and non-perishable foods and other goods and services. Besides, she helped to write all the contracts. She assisted with the planning and conducted most of the training meetings.

However, despite her many attributes, the way she talked down to the county program staff was one of her major shortcomings. She was mean-spirited and very domineering. While acting as AAA Director, she demonstrated how domineering she could be. Her behavior exhibited that she viewed the AAA Director's position as being the bully pulpit. Being aware that some of the county's aging staff did not like her, one would have assumed she would have been more lenient, but instead, Camilla was raising hell about everything she was displeased with.

Camilla was an attractive 46-year-old light-brown complexion female. She stood 5'11" with her weight in proportion to her height. She wore her hair cut in a cute short style. She was married and the mother of four children.

As time passed and everyone waited to see who would get the appointment, Camilla continued to show confidence that she would be the next AAA Director. Finally, after more than two months, the personnel committee members met one morning and reached an agreement.

Angela's supporters had spent numerous hours calling many of the other Commission members, asking for their support.

After their morning meeting had adjourned, several committee members stopped by Angela's office and whispered congratulations. That afternoon, around 1:30 p.m., the 19-member executive committee met. However, when the personnel committee announced their choice, a conflict developed between Scott County Commissioners. One of the personnel committee members who served as a proxy for Commissioner Miller supported Angela for the appointment. Several of the Republican County Commissioners were not pleased with his decision because they were backing Susan's choice, and that was Camilla. Even after they had been told about Camilla's bullying statement, they were still upset that he had gone against their wishes and voted for another candidate.

The Republican County Commissioners who had worked with Susan supporting Camilla's appointment were so upset they demanded a recount but could not get the motion passed. Finally, after a couple of hours, the chairman and other members supporting Angela got the votes they needed, which was 16-3.

While the Planning Commission staff watched and waited, those who were aware that several commissioners had stopped by Angela's office after the morning meeting, believed she had gotten the appointment. However, those who had supported Camilla believed that she had gotten the appointment.

Finally, after the battle was over, the chairman and the vice-chairman stopped by Angela's office closed the door, and stated,' *"Semper Fi,"*

"Semper Fi," Angela responded with the pride of a US Marine. They didn't need to say anything else. One after the other, executive committee members stopped by Angela's office to congratulate her.

Chapter – Eleven

UNCONTROLLABLE RAGE

Seeing the executive committee members going in and out of Angela's office with smiles, it is evident to all the staff that Angela was the new AAA Director. Several staff members then came to her office to congratulate her. Shortly afterward, Camilla stormed into Angela's office, outraged and beside herself with anger.

"Why are you just sitting there?" She yelled in anger.

Seeing Camilla's rage, Angela was calm and decided not to say anything that would fuel the fire.

Furiously Camilla yelled, *"So, they chose you over me."*

Hesitating, Angela calmly said, *"Yes."*

After Camilla shouted a few other negative comments, she hurriedly left and headed down the hall to Mr. Percy's office. Mr. Percy and a group of executive committee members were behind closed doors discussing how the votes had gone and what was said after telling the opposing members about Camilla's threatening comments. At that moment, without knocking, Camilla shoved the door open and walked in. She immediately started yelling at the executive committee members. She informed the committee members that it wasn't over and they would be sorry for their decision. When they asked her to leave, she continued shouting threatening remarks.

"Y'all will be sorry, I promise." She angrily yelled.

Her outburst was loud enough to be heard by everyone in the office. She behaved in a manner no one would have ever expected. After she had displayed her bitterness, she turned and walked out, slamming the door so hard that it caused the pictures on the wall in the hallway to become misaligned. She then went into her office got her purse, and left.

The following day she did not come in; dates on letters showed that she had gone to the Equal Employment Opportunity Commission (EEOC) and filed a discrimination grievance. Several days later, an EEOC representative was in the office to talk to Mr. Percy. Angela was not disturbed about the visit, for she was familiar with all of the EEO and Affirmative Action (AA) Laws. She served as the Equal Opportunity Advisor (EOA) for her military unit and graduated from the Defense Equal Opportunity Management Institute, Patrick Air Force Base. As a trained professional EOA, Angela knew that Camilla did not have a case, but EEOC would still investigate the claim.

In less than ten days after Camilla had filed a discrimination claim, an EEOC representative had investigated and notified her that the Commission had not discriminated against her. Their letter was very disturbing to Camilla, and she showed it in every action. Mr. Percy suggested that she take some time off to get herself together, but she refused.

To ease her pain and frustration, she went to the extreme trying to outdo Angela in every area. When Angela received congratulatory flowers and cards, Camilla would order a much larger, expensive floral arrangement for herself and, send herself several congratulatory cards. Her behavior was extremely irrational; staff members didn't know how to deal with her; still, they made every effort to put up with her. Finally, after some time had gone by, several staff members confronted Camilla and attempted to reason with her. They told her they understood her disappointment, but her irrational behavior had demonstrated her inability to deal with job difficulties. They also informed her that they would go to the executive committee and ask to have her dismissed if her malicious behavior didn't cease. These were painful remarks coming from people she had known for years. As time passed, Camilla's overt negative behavior ceased. She would come to work each day wearing a cheerful smile, speaking to all the staff, and apologizing for her past bad behavior. She would go to Angela's office and pretend to be offering assistance, but when Angela would ask for specific help, Camilla would pretend to be oblivious. She would always tell Angela that Susan had never involved her in the task.

Camilla went so far as to persuade Lynette to take her side and refuse to work with Angela. However, when they reached out to the other aging staff and tried to persuade them to challenge Angela's authority, they were unsuccessful. The other staff consisted of a program para-legal, who worked with an attorney at the University of Alabama; the program Ombudsman; the computer programmer; and the Medicaid Waiver employees; Valeria, Brenda, Evelyn, Felicia, Gloria, Shelley, and Belinda. Valeria's primary job was to input data on the computer and work with the home health care agencies that provided services to their elderly clients.

Realizing what Camilla and Lynette were trying to do, Angela started seeking help from other sources. She started reading every federal and state guideline she could get her hands on. In addition, she stayed in prayer, reading the words written in *Matthew 7, 'Ask and it will be given to you; seek and you will find; knock, and it will be opened to you. For everyone who asks receives, and he who seeks finds.'*

Believing strongly in God's word, God did not fail her. A couple of years earlier, Angela had established a relationship with a gentleman at the Administration on Aging (AOA), who also had a career in writing and publishing. The two had exchanged ideas about a book Angela was writing and trying to get published. The gentleman had read several chapters and was giving Angela feedback on areas she needed to work on. However, after being appointed AAA Director, Angela put the manuscript aside to deal with job problems. Not having talked with her in several months, the gentleman called to check on her writing. She told him about her job appointment and the difficulties she was being confronted with. He immediately took it upon himself to see that Angela got the support needed. He put her in contact with AAA Directors and state agencies throughout the United States. She didn't have to call them; they called her.

Grace, the aging program secretary, was a knowledgeable White female in her mid-sixties. She was exceptional in her job duties. Knowing the difficulties Angela had to contend with, Grace prepared all the reports, got Angela's signature, and mailed the reports on time. She continued to perform her duties just as she had always done.

Together with Grace, Valeria was in the office all day, and as a result, they quickly bonded. In addition to their discussions about job-related issues, they talked about their Christian faith and trust in God.

As time passed, after Camilla realized she would not be able to convince the other program staff to rebel and stop performing their duties, Camilla sought help from Susan.

Being disappointed that Camilla had not gotten the job, Susan was now facing a barrier she had not expected. Had Camilla been appointed, Susan and Scott County Republican County Commissioners would have been able to take the program and set it up in Scott County as an independent entity. But with Angela now in the position, Susan was faced with fighting against a person she had previously held high regard for. Though she and Angela had talked many times about the cost of having AAAs under the Council of Governments, Angela had never given Susan any reason to believe she thought it was a great idea.

Being disappointed that her plot had failed, Susan started making it difficult for Angela to obtain help from COA. She instructed the receptionist to direct all of Angela's phone calls to her office, regardless of the purpose of the calls. Being aware of the instructions given and knowing the problems Susan was trying to impose on Angela put several of the COA staff members in a position of having to take Angela's side. To protect themselves they would call Angela at home to fill her in on what was going on and answer any questions she had.

The first three and a half months as AAA Director was very challenging. Angela worked long hours administering the Senior Employment

Program, the employment services contracts, the Medicaid Waiver Program, and the Aging Program. During that time and the months that followed, Angela was putting all of her trust in God. She would start her mornings off reading the 23rd Psalms. The words gave her the peace she needed to get through each day.

Daily, Valeria would come into Angela's office with words to brighten her spirit. She would always compliment Angela by telling her that she handled the job and stress like a true Marine. During one of their conversations, Angela told Valeria that she now understood the meaning of the phrase, *'out of a frying pan and into a hot skillet.'*

After nearly five months, the executive committee appointed Valeria as the Director of, the Senior Employment Program. Angela was very pleased, for Valeria had been very supportive of her while she was having to deal with the stress of administering all of the programs.

During the time Angela was administering all the programs, Camilla and Lynette did everything they could to undermine and sabotage every effort she made. Angela was unable to get any information or productive work from either of them. She had once thought she could win them over by including them in every aspect of administering the programs and letting them know how much she needed their help. She was hoping they could restore the relationship they had once shared, but they were both determined to create problems.

Every day, Angela was confronted with a problem, either in-house or in the counties. However, not all of the issues were related to the aging program. Approximately eight months after becoming AAA Director, Angela started receiving resumes. Considering there were no vacancies, she did not take the time to review them. One morning while standing in Grace's office chatting, Grace asked about the resumes. She then pulled two resumes from the files and gave them to Angela. When Angela started reading the cover letters, she started smiling. Being aware that the resumes were from two of Angela's former co-workers, Grace began to chuckle.

"I could see that the three of you once worked together," Grace said.

"We did."

"It appears they're asking you for a job."

"Yeah, they are."

Angela then gave the letters back to Grace to file.

"I get the impression you don't want to talk about them."

"I will some other time, but I must say, it's good to see that one does reap what they sow."

A month later, Angela was served with a subpoena to testify on behalf of the two women who had the sent resumes. Angela was ecstatic that these women would apply for employment with her, and they had the audacity to ask her to testify against Ms. Henderson on their behalf. It was evident to Angela that Ms. Henderson had been getting rid of people she didn't trust. It was gratifying to Angela to see these were the same women who had told lies about her while she was with the agency. Angela smiled when she thought of the words written in *Galatians 6: 7*, *"Do not be deceived. God is not mocked: for whatever a man sows, that he will also reap."*

Later that day, after telling Valeria about the resumes and the subpoena, Valeria laughed and said, *"I can see Ms. Henderson is still inflicting pain on people who work for her."*

"Yes, she is," Angela said with laughter.

"Have you thought about what you're going to say?"

"I could say a great deal, but Ms. Henderson and I are now counterparts."

Again Valeria started laughing; *"Can you believe that? I bet she never envisioned you would one day become her equal."*

"That is something to think about," Angela said. *"But then again, I never envision becoming an AAA Director."*

Chapter – Twelve

OVERSPENDING PLOT

The following week Angela reported to the attorneys' office to give her deposition. She was seated at a large table with her two former co-workers, their attorneys, and Ms. Henderson. After each attorney made a brief statement of what they wanted to uncover, they began asking Angela questions. With each question, regardless of how it was worded or which attorney asked the question, Angela disclaimed having any firsthand knowledge of what they were trying to uncover. After they had concluded the two-hour deposition, Angela and Ms. Henderson stood outside talking. In light of the fact Ms. Henderson and Angela had previously had their differences, they were now colleagues. Though it was never mentioned during their conversation, Ms. Henderson was aware of some of the problems Angela was having to contend with. Knowing that Ms. Henderson had taken programs from the Planning Commission years earlier, Scott County officials were communicating with her to gain knowledge and support. They were working on behalf of Susan since Susan was unable to communicate with Ms. Henderson. Ms. Henderson had publicly made her feelings known about her disapproval of Susan's appointment as COA Deputy Director.

As time passed, having always wanted to pull the aging program from under the Commission, Susan had hoped that Camilla would have been appointed AAA Director. However, after that failure, she realized her only choice was to accomplish the task without Camilla's help, so she began putting forth greater effort to take the aging program.

As COA Deputy Director, Susan carried on as if her primary responsibilities included interfering with the Commission's affairs. Being aware of Susan's anger with the Commission, the COA staff realized what she was doing and decided not to allow her to use them. Susan went so far as to instruct the finance department to give her all of the Commission funding requests. She intended to hold the request forms and force the Commission to wait. Knowing her intentions, the department staff would process the reports, prepare the checks, and take everything to Commissioner Rucker for his signature. Their routine procedure was to mail all the checks and other information out, but Susan had ordered them to give her everything relating to the Commission. After they had done everything she had instructed them to do, they would call Angela and let her know the checks were ready. This would result in Angela driving 224 miles round trip to Montgomery and stopping in to chat with Commissioner Rucker. On her way out, she would just so happen to remember to ask if the checks had been processed. Commissioner Rucker would then ask one of the secretaries to look for the check(s) in Susan's office.

As time passed, Susan's inability to gain the support of all of the COA Staff, she reached out to Tammie, her administrative assistant. Tammie was an attractive, 42-year-old, dark brown-complexion female. She stood approximately 5'11" tall, with her weight in proportion to her height. She had been with the State Commission for more than eighteen years as the administrative assistant to the former Commissioner. She was hungry for recognition and power, and having Susan onboard, presented her with the opportunity to gain the recognition she had long desired. She was known for being conniving and pretentious and with Susan and Dr. Tucker, she could now put those skills into use. She praised Susan and Commissioner Rucker daily and offered her assistance over and above her duties. Under the former Commissioner, Tammie had never had the privilege of deviating far from her assigned role. However, working with Commissioner Rucker and Susan, Tammie now had the opportunity to show that she could be an outstanding asset.

Having failed at getting the other COA staff assistance in carrying out her plot, Susan got Tammie involved. One of the jobs Susan got Tammie's assistance in was to find something to criticize Angela for. To accomplish that goal, Tammie had to intrude on the roles of other staff; but the other staff did not appreciate her involvement. To prevent Tammie from succeeding, they kept Angela informed about everything Tammie was trying to do.

Another plot Tammie and Susan came up with was to have Tammie make a site monitoring visit to the Planning Commission. Tammie's objective was to find anything she could write up as a negative comment. However, when Angela's COA supporters learned about the scheduled monitoring visit, they called and told Angela. Angela then called Commissioner Rucker and asked him for a letter clarifying what COA needed. While they were talking, Commissioner Rucker asked the financial officer to come in and speak with Angela to explain what they asking for. He then pushed the speaker's bottom so the three of them could talk. The financial officer pretended to be stunned when Angela told him that Tammie was scheduled to visit the Commission, but Tammie had not given her a reason for the visit and the information she would want to review. The financial officer then told Angela that his department was unaware of any need for information. He then explained to Commissioner Rucker the procedures they would follow before making a site visit. Upon hearing this, Commissioner Rucker called Tammie to his office and told her, in the presence of the finance officer, that the visit was unnecessary.

Despite the problems Angela was having with Susan, Camilla, and Lynette she enjoyed some pleasures. The contractor that provided the meals for the seniors in the centers around the state was still trying to influence the Planning Commission to enter a food service contract with them. They tried to entice Angela in many ways: The company sales representatives frequently invited Angela to lunch and other affairs. She was invited to attend the regional nutrition conferences the business held for its clients'. At the conferences, the sales representatives ensured that Angela was treated with the utmost respect and attention. The reason was, that the other twelve AAA Directors were already in their pocket, and they were trying to get the Commission to join the group. At dinners and other social gatherings, Angela was always seated between a salesman and one of the business lobbyists. They made sure she was pleased with everything. Angela was treated to dinner at the Red Diamond Hotel in Tennessee. Dining on the top floor gave you a spectacular view of the surrounding area. She was also treated to dinner cruises aboard the General Marco Showboat. Everywhere she went she received special treatment. At the newly built Birmingham Turf Club, Angela was instructed to go to the VIP parking, where a valet would take her car and park it, then an escort would meet her and take her to the clubhouse. To protect herself from criticism Angela would always invite other Commission staff to accompany her. She shared the fruits of her special honor with other Commission staff who wanted to partake. It was amazing the trouble the food service business went through and the money they were willing to spend to get the Commission food service contract, but Angela never gave in. The amusing part about all of their attempts to influence Angela was, that Susan was always present. To see Angela and Susan interact with each other on those occasions, one would never have believed they had become adversaries. The two would laugh together and speak well of each other as they had done while Susan was still with the Commission. People who knew how Susan felt about Angela's appointment would caution Angela, telling her to be careful because Susan was like a snake in the grass. She could smile in your face while trying to stab you in the back. But Angela wasn't troubled by that, considering she had worked with Ms. Henderson, who was an expert in that area.

As time passed, seeing that Susan's plans to take the aging program were not working, Camilla's frustration increased and she became more vindictive. Her antagonism grew to the point she would rather have seen the program destroyed if she couldn't be the AAA Director. On several occasions, Angela spoke with Mr. Percy about the things and behaviors Camilla and Lynette were doing to challenge her authority. She presented him with documentation sufficient to terminate both of them, but he refused to take any action. Being a leader who couldn't handle stress, he got to the point where he was unwilling to talk with Angela about the problems she was having with Camilla and Lynette.

Among Camilla's various duties was the management of the food and equipment services contracts. If a problem arose, she would discuss the situation with Angela, and they would decide on the course of action needed to resolve the problem. After writing up the information to send to the county(s) or vendors, Camilla would bring the letter to Angela for her signature.

Out of spitefulness, Camilla came up with a plot that would cause the nutritious side of the program to go into overspending. She cunningly altered the food supplies contracts months after Angela had approved them. She then told the county coordinators that COA had sent Angela a letter informing her that the Commission could get additional funds if she could come up with a plan to spend the money in a given period. Camilla suggested that, since the money was to be used for nutrition, they could allow the seniors to eat exceptionally well for as long as the money lasted. The county coordinators were extremely pleased; they could now offer meals they had only dreamed of. Camilla went so far as to take on the responsibility of revising the county's meal plans showing the new food choices. She then hid them to make sure Angela would not see the changes. Unfortunately, the county coordinators had no idea that Camilla was getting them to help her implement a plot to send the program into overspending. Not being aware of the problems Angela was having in-house with Camilla, they never considered verifying the changes Camilla had made.

Having carried out as much damage as she could, Camilla called Angela one evening and told her that she needed to take leave to go and see about her sick father, who was near death. Hearing this, Angela was surprised, for Camilla had told her that her father had died years earlier.

As weeks passed, the food suppliers were extremely pleased. They were making more money due to the types of foods being ordered. The counties were now purchasing more expensive food items. Camilla's actions were creating an overspending of $25K each month.

Camilla was gone for an extended period without leaving information as to how she could be reached. During her absence, when Angela needed information she thought Lynette could provide, Lynette would always pretend as if she didn't know the answer. Suspecting that Lynette and Camilla were working together, Angela sought to obtain needed information from the county coordinators. She was fortunate; the ties she had established in her former position aided her in getting things accomplished. The county coordinators were eager to assist Angela. You could say they were competing with each other trying to see who could be most helpful. They would offer their assistance in any area Angela needed help in. However, Angela felt more comfortable calling on Clara, the Clair County Coordinator. Clara was by far the most successful of the five. She was always forthright and very seldom beat around the bush. Angela referred to Clara as a straight shooter. Knowing this, Angela would communicate with Clara more often than she would with the other four county coordinators.

During a conversation between Angela and Clara regarding the usage of Clair County participants' contributions, Clara expressed her disappointment. Clara believed that her efforts to bring in more money were being defeated. She complained about not being allowed to keep the funds she was raising. Angela listened but said very little, for she did not understand the problem Clara was trying to tell her about. However, after returning to her office, Angela pulled several of Clair County's monthly funding requests and expense reports and Clara's annual proposal. After reviewing and analyzing the information, Angela could see what Clara was trying to tell her. It could easily be seen that Clara's fundraising efforts were not benefiting her program.

Each county prepared an annual proposal showing the services they would provide and the projected cost of those services. Their budgets showed their local, federal, and state dollars and the contributions and small grants they expected to receive. The federal and state funds they received were based on a formula that took into account; the county's population, race, poverty level, and the percentage of people sixty years and older. Unfortunately, while Susan was AAA Director, the federal and state dollars Clara had been awarded had always decreased because of the contributions and other small grants Clara received. Viewing this, Angela could see that Clara's hard work was not paying off, and it appeared that all of her efforts were in vain. Further review of documents relating to the other counties showed they were benefitting from Clara's hard work. After discovering this, Angela had each county coordinator revise their budgets. The revisions allowed them to keep the federal and state dollars they were awarded in their grant proposal and use the contributions and other funds raised to improve and expand the services.

With the Commission's grant writing support, Clara was able to obtain assistance in writing several proposals and receiving small grants. With the money from the grants and the contributions, Clara was able to make some needed improvements. She remodeled several of her county senior centers and purchased a new 16-passenger transportation van. Angela had taught Clara how to keep the funds she raised and not lose the federal dollars she was awarded. This made Clara and her county officials very happy.

After getting all the county's revised budgets, Angela realized that the county coordinators' knowledge was limited to what they were learning from the other county coordinators and center managers around the state. To allow them to see how other states ran their programs, Angela believed it would be necessary for them to attend national conventions where they could meet and learn from other service providers. After talking to the county coordinators about the conventions, she learned they did not have the money to attend. After pondering over the situation for several days, Angela felt the need to fund the trips for the coordinators and their assistants. However, after calculating the money needed, she realized that her budget could not support the trip for all of them.

As the deadline for registration was rapidly approaching, Angela remembered that Susan was always out of town attending conventions.

Considering this was not a question she could call and ask Susan about, she decided to review several budgets and expense reports from previous years. She discovered that most of Susan's overspending was due to the expense of the trips she took. That was obvious because the money Susan had put into her training and travel line items was far less than the money reported on her expense sheets. Angela laughed upon realizing that Susan had mismanaged the program funds for her travel and entertainment expenses. After further reviewing the previous year's budgets, she was able to see that the aging program had always paid a large amount of money into the in-direct pool. This was one of the problems Susan had always complained about. The money in those three line items; training, travel, and the in-direct pool, stirred up Angela's desire to dig deeper and understand the financial problems. She looked at the aging program spending and reviewed the expenditures of the money paid in indirect costs. After reviewing the expenses covered under the in-direct category, Angela could see that the Commission used an excessive amount of money for public relations. This was a problem the executive committee constantly criticized Mr. Percy about. The cost of printing and mailing was extremely high. The Commission mailed out thousands of publications to agencies throughout the United States. Seeing this, Angela began to understand some of the problems the other division directors complained about. After pondering over her findings, she decided to go to the executive director for financial help.

Chapter – Thirteen

PLOT DISCOVERED

The following day Angela went to Mr. Percy and asked for the money needed to take the county coordinators to the conference. She told him how helpful it would be for them to learn how other states operated their programs. Angela then threw in a few remarks concerning the money the aging program paid in the in-direct pool in contrast to the administrative support they received from the Commission's administrative support staff. After much discussion, Mr. Percy agreed to give her the money she requested.

Their first trip was to Louisville, Kentucky, to attend the National Nutrition Service Providers Conference. The driving there and back was as much fun as the conference activities. She and the county coordinators and their assistants traveled in three of the Commission vehicles. They tailgated and played the game of catch-up on the highway. As they passed each other, they would hold up a sign in the window asking, 'Who is the leader now.' Though they were all mature women, some with grandchildren, they were like teenagers in their parents' cars. They stopped for gas and ate their meals at truck stops. They had a ball chatting with the drivers of the 18-wheelers. When they were getting back on the road, they warned the drivers of the 18-wheelers to get out of the way if they saw the Commission vehicles coming. The drivers of the 18-wheelers teased them by notifying other drivers to be on the lookout for the ladies in grey company vehicles.

Though the trip was primarily for the coordinators and their assistants, Angela had allowed Lynette to come along. Having learned about the trip from Lynette, Camilla had called Angela before they left Birmingham and asked if she could attend the conference. Angela took it as a joke, for she hadn't heard from Camilla in nearly three months. However, after giving Camilla's request much consideration, she decided it would be a great opportunity to get Camilla and Lynette together and get to the bottom of some of the problems.

After they had arrived at the hotel and unpacked, they all met in Angela's suite for a meeting. Once the meeting was over, Angela told Camilla and Lynette to stay behind so that they could discuss some business. As soon as they were alone and Angela brought up the subject of their behavior, Camilla and Lynette took the position that Angela's mistrust of them caused all the problems. They both talked continually, accusing Angela of mimicking Ms. Henderson. Though it was not flattering, Angela chuckled.

"So that's how I sound to you. Well.., I did learn a lot while employed with her."

"It's obvious," Camilla said with a giggle.

As they continued talking, Angela calmly sat, listening to their arrogant statements about why they had taken certain actions. Then Angela decided they had talked enough. At that point, she lit into them and chewed them out like a Marine Corps Drill Sergeant speaking to recruits. She told Camilla that if she didn't report to work the following Monday, she would have her fired. Angela told her that she would bypass Mr. Percy and go directly to the executive committee. In an arrogant tone, Angela told the two that she had taken as much of their shit as she was willing to accept. Angela then smiled and told them she was ready to show them what working for Ms. Henderson would be like. Angela then picked up her purse and walked out, leaving the two behind, looking at each other with a smirked expression.

Throughout the conference, they attended various training meetings and activities. The county coordinators learned a great deal of information they could take back and implement in their counties. The trip allowed them to meet people from across the United States.

The following Monday, Camilla reported to work. She immediately started making out her weekly schedule of things she was planning to do. Angela had already made out work schedules for Camilla and Lynette, but her schedule required them to stay in the office and prepare a job task description handbook. The handbook was to cover everything they did, day by day and hour by hour. When she called them in and gave them the schedule and the instructions, they both appeared stunned that she would ask them to perform such a task. They both began telling her where she could obtain the information she was requesting. Angela looked at them as if she didn't hear them. She then told them that she wanted the information from them no later than the close of business on Wednesday. She then walked out of her office, leaving the two standing there.

As they prepared the information, Angela could hear the typewriters at work. Finally, after hours of typing, Lynette brought a typed outline in, showing what she did. Angela took the sheets and instructed Lynette to sit as she reviewed the information. As Angela read and marked up the information with a red pen, Lynette sat gazing with a sarcastic look. Many of the comments Angela was writing were statements like; not clear, not enough information, regulations needed, and the time required to accomplish the task. After Angela had finished, she gave the sheets back to Lynette and told her to add more, giving her specific instructions explaining; who, what, when, where, and why.

"*Why is that necessary?*" Lynette asked in a discourteous tone.

Angela told her that she could never do her job with such meager information. From the expression on Lynette's face, Angela could sense that Lynette understood what she was implying. As Lynette was reading over the comments, she frowned and shook her head, showing that she was not pleased.

"Oh well," Lynette said as she was walking out.

Before being led astray by Camilla, Lynette was thought of, as a nice friendly person, but after getting caught up in Camilla and Susan's battle to take the aging program she became equally difficult to get along with.

Lynette was an attractive, 40-year-old light complexion, Black female with long red hair that hung down her back. Her physical size and height drew attention; she was tall and extremely thin. She was known for dressing very flamboyantly during different holiday seasons. On that particular day, she was wearing an outfit that Angela would normally have complimented her on, but because of the things going on, Angela was more in a chastising mood.

An hour later, Camilla brought her information to Angela and placed the papers in Angela's inbox.

"Go ahead and have a seat. I want to go over the information while you're here."

"I have something to do," Camilla said as she turned to walk out.

"No! You don't. Nothing is more important than this."

Camilla then turned and stared at Angela but refused to sit down. Seeing the expression on Camellia's face, Angela said sternly. *"Continue standing if you wish."*

At that moment, Camilla sat down, crossed her legs, folded her arms, and stared at Angela.

"Good! Now that I have your attention, I'll review what you have prepared."

As Camilla sat staring, Angela proceeded to read over the information. As she read, she wrote numerous comments. After she finished, she gave the papers back to Camilla and told her to read over the sheets while she made a phone call. After Angela had finished her call, she turned and asked Camilla if she understood the comments. From the various facial expressions Camilla displayed, Angela could tell she had gotten the best of Camilla. She then instructed Camilla to make all the changes and provide more details.

Wednesday afternoon, around 3:30 p.m., after completing the task, Camilla and Lynette came to Angela's office together and gave her the information. As Angela flipped through the pages she could see that the documents had been well prepared, with the detailed information she had requested. It was apparent they expected Angela to make comments about the documents, but she didn't. She then thanked them and put the documents in her briefcase. The two then asked why she had required them to perform the task. Angela looked at them with a stern look, then said: *"If either of you play that dumb, incompetent shit on me again, I will go directly to the executive committee to have you fired!"*

She then turned, picked up a document from her tray, and began reviewing it.

Camilla and Lynette were both aware that the program was going into overspending. They were hoping Angela would not discover the problem until enough damage had been carried out.

A week later, after getting to work one morning, Judy, the accountant, came to Angela and asked why the food supply companies were billing for such large amounts of money. Judy explained that this had been occurring for several months. Being a bit puzzled, Angela asked Judy for clarification. While Judy had gone back to her office to get the invoices, Angela went to the conference room to get a cup of coffee. As they sat at the conference room table looking at the invoices, Angela could see that there was something wrong. She then called Grace and asked her to pull certain documents and bring them to the conference room. After looking at the reports, she could see the differences in the signature and the dates signed. Looking at the original meal plans, she discovered that the food items the counties were ordering were different from those in the plans. Angela was shocked as she stared at the changes Camilla had made. Judy could see that Angela was upset when she put her elbows on the table and her hands over her face, and started shaking her head. Seeing the amount of money in quarterly overspending was truly shocking to Angela.

"Don't let them get away with this," Judy said as she reached over and embraced Angela.

"I know you'll fix the problem," Judy said.

Once Angela had regained her composure, she and Judy stayed in the conference room, discussing how she would handle the situation. After talking a while longer, they decided to hide all the documents in one of the division directors' offices before going back to their office.

Later that afternoon after Angela had prayed about the situation and spiritually equipped her mind, she called Camilla in to go over the findings. Camilla first attempted to disclaim altering the contracts, but Angela refused to accept the lie.

"Well!" Camilla said with a cunning smile on her face. *"What are you going to do about it?"*

Not wanting to let Camilla get the best of her and knowing Mr. Percy would not allow her to take corrective actions, Angela told Camilla that she would take care of the problem.

Angela spent the next several days visiting the county programs trying to get a clearer picture of what had taken place. She learned from talking to the county coordinators that Camilla had talked them into revising their menus. She also learned that the food choices had been made by Camellia. To play it off, Angela joked about it, for she didn't want the county coordinators to know about the problems she was having to deal with.

During Angela's visit to Clair County, she asked Clara how the seniors enjoyed the new food items. Clara told her that, at first, the seniors were excited to have the opportunity to try something different, but after several weeks had passed, they began complaining and asking when they were going back to their old menus.

"You know how it is," Clara said. *"Everyone likes something new every once in a while, but most older people like sticking to foods they are accustomed to."*

Clara and Angela agreed that older people enjoyed eating the foods they were brought up eating. After joking about the different foods, Angela suggested they return to the original menus.

The altered menus had the seniors eating croissants, prime rib roast, steaks, lamb chops, porterhouse roast, asparagus and broccoli casseroles, and various uncommon desserts such as tiramisu and key line pies. Several food items were not common among the food supply companies; they had to order those items from outside of the region.

Angela was fortunate; the seniors missed having the everyday foods they enjoyed. Their former menus included; homemade rolls, biscuits, cornbread, baked chicken, roast beef, meatloaf, fresh vegetables, peach, apple, blackberry cobblers, and sweet potato pies. The changes to the menu resulted in a decrease in the number of seniors coming in daily.

During Angela's conversations with the county coordinators, she learned they were unaware that she had not approved the menu changes. Several county coordinators asked Angela if she could spend all the money Camilla had told them about. Without giving them a clear-cut answer, Angela smiled. She chose not to tell them that Camilla had lied to get them to help her send the program into overspending. Knowing what she had to do, Angela asked the county coordinators for their help. She suggested they start using the old menu to get their participant's daily numbers back up. To be sure she was doing the right thing, she asked the coordinators to schedule a meeting with the participants so she could get their feedback.

On the day of the first meeting held in Clair County, Angela began asking the seniors for their help. The seniors listened as she gave them some details and told them it was a big misunderstanding. Hearing of the problems she was being confronted with, they all seemed happy to have the opportunity to help. When they got on the subject of fancy foods, several of the seniors responded and told her that they wanted to go back to their old menus. They all then raised their hands in agreement.

After going to each county and getting the same feedback from the seniors, Angela was faced with having to amend the contracts with the vendors. Instead of resolving the problem by phone, Angela went directly to the supplier for a face-to-face meeting. Before meeting with the suppliers, Angela went through the contracts, line by line, to ensure there was a way out. She was fortunate; an adequate protection clause in the contracts gave the Commission options without taking the contractors' rights away.

On the day of her visits to the supplier, she signed out, stating that she would be out of the office all day, but did not say where she was going. After getting in the car, she realized she had left some information behind. This resulted in her having to go back upstairs. As she walked by Camilla and Lynette's office, she noticed neither was present. Being a bit curious and not being able to trust them Angela asked Grace if she knew their whereabouts. Grace told her that the two had walked by her office moments earlier, but neither said anything. As Angela was leaving for the second time she checked to see if either had signed out. Seeing that they had not, she concluded that they were taking a break. Walking by the ladies' room Angela decided to stop in before getting on the road. Standing in front of the mirror, thinking of how she would appear before the vendors, she overheard laughter coming from the restroom. As she listened closely, she realized it was Lynette and Camilla. They were laughing about the overspending problem.

As she stood listening, she overheard Camilla say; *"Let's see if she can get her ass out of this one."*

Angela remained silent, listening to the rest of their conversation. Upon hearing the paper towel rack, Angela quickly moved to the entrance, opened the door, and said loud enough for them to hear: 'Let's talk about it later.'

Upon entering the restroom and seeing the look on their faces she could tell they were surprised to see her.

"I had to come back to get a document." She told them, as she was going into one of the restroom stalls.

Chapter – Fourteen

PROGRAM ABANDONED

A couple of days later, several men from the different food supply companies showed up for an early morning meeting Angela had arranged with their companies. Considering the time and the fact she had a small catering business, she had prepared breakfast for them. After they had eaten and chatted for a while, they got busy working on a plan to help alleviate the problem she was facing.

During her visits to the companies, she had gone directly to the top managers and told them the problems she was dealing with. She provided them with some details and asked them to review the data to see how things would work out with the proposed changes.

Angela believed that most people who were climbing the corporate ladder would understand. Being a military woman also gave her some clout, and she used that to her advantage. During those years, most men had served time in one of the military branches. Angela was also a praying woman, and she had turned the problem over to God and was now acting on faith after having done all she could do.

While the men worked, Angela sat quietly in the conference room, working on other problems. After several hours had gone by and the noise from the calculators had ceased, Angela had gotten the changes she needed to solve the problem. With the changes, the food supply companies lost after having made the earlier changes Camilla had requested.

After the men left, Angela walked down the hill and sat in the park praying, thanking God for His goodness. Upon returning to her office, she got Grace to call and schedule a meeting with the county coordinators. Two days later, Angela was having lunch with the county coordinators and telling them about the changes and the things she needed their help with. She had earlier asked them to prepare an inventory of everything they had in stock. After they had talked and agreed on what they needed to do, they went back to their respective counties and made a list of the things they would keep. To show their willingness to assist, they called each other to determine who needed what. After receiving the information from the county coordinators, Angela got with Camilla and Lynette and set up times for them to go out to the counties, gather the non-perishable foods and supplies, and transport them where needed. They had to travel throughout the five counties, going from one senior center to another. In some cases, they traveled more than three hundred miles per day.

Angela had rented two cargo vans and hired men to drive the vans and handle the dropping off and picking up to counteract any grievance from Camilla and Lynette. All Camilla and Lynette were required to do was ride along and show the men where to go. Angela had instructed the men not to allow Camilla nor Lynette to do any of the labor. The job entailed moving containers of paper goods, disposable eating utensils, canned foods, and other items used in food services. Camilla had ordered large quantities of food and disposable items, despite the fact they were not needed. Getting all the items transported around took Camilla and Lynette a week to complete the job.

After Angela had solved the meal problems, she canceled all unnecessary traveling and conferences and rescheduled all of the county coordinator's meetings. Whereas previous meetings were held in restaurants or county country clubs, Angela decided to have the meetings at the Commission. Camilla and Lynette whispered, saying Angela was making a bad decision, but to their surprise, the county coordinators loved the idea. The coordinators got to show off their cooking skills; they would bring in one of their favorite dishes to share. Angela made many changes that cut spending and allowed her to start building up funds to carry over to the next program year. Genesis 50-20, *but as for you, you meant evil against me, but God meant it for good."*

As time passed, other unforeseen problems began to emerge that affected not only the Commission but all of the councils of governments. The State Commission on Aging was entering a phase of a financial shortfall. Though the problem had been brought to Commissioner Rucker's attention, he did not understand the significance of the problem. He had inherited a state department filled with financial problems, but neither he nor Susan had taken the time to learn their jobs and find out what was going on. They were both too busy getting involved with other issues. Commissioner Rucker was busy traveling around the state, making speeches about the great man Governor Hanson was. At the same time, Susan was busy putting her efforts into taking the aging program from the Planning Commission.

They had been in their jobs no more than twenty-six months when the financial problem was brought to Commissioner Rucker's attention. One afternoon after leaving the Governor's cabinet meeting, Commissioner Rucker was standing in the corridor chatting with several cabinet members when the state budget director pulled him aside and gave him the bad news. He was told that the State Commission on Aging did not have sufficient matching funds to meet its financial obligations for the remaining months of the year. The budget director explained that the state matching funds that had been set aside to match the Federal Medicaid Waiver Program dollars had been used to match other federal programs. As Commissioner Rucker listened, the budget director told him that the Waiver Program funded critical care services for frail homebound elderly. He went so far as to give Commissioner Rucker a bit of history regarding the Waiver Program. He explained that the State Commission on Aging received one-third 1/3 of the federal dollars, and the State Welfare Agency (SWA) received 2/3. This financial information was a foreign language to Commissioner Rucker, for he had come into a state cabinet position believing that everything was working out well.

After coming to an understanding and realizing the problem his department was facing, Commissioner Rucker did what many employees would do; he went directly to the Governor. The Governor then called on the assistance of other cabinet heads to help solve the problem.

Unfortunately, Commissioner Rucker was unaware that the Commissioner of the State Welfare Agency (SWA) wanted the entire Waiver Program, and he saw this as an opportunity to take it. During the meeting, Commissioner Nelson offered to help solve the problem by taking over the whole Waiver Program. The problem with his offer was, that the welfare agency would be in total control of the program, eliminating the participation of the Council of Governments/AAA. Not comprehending the problems that would be brought on, Commissioner Rucker did not consult with his staff or any of the Council of Government Executive or AAAs. Believing he had the right to make the decision, he abandoned control of the Waiver Program, giving it to the State Welfare Agency Commissioner Rucker was unaware that Commissioner Nelson was setting him up with no intention of ever giving the program back. Further, the State Welfare Agency would be able to demonstrate that they were better qualified to manage the entire program.

Commissioner Rucker's trust in the State Welfare Commissioner could have resulted in COA losing millions of dollars in federal Medicaid Waiver funds. He didn't realize the trouble he was putting COA staff in by giving up the Waiver Program. Not only was he getting rid of members of his staff, but he was also cutting out some of the AAA and COG employees and the staff of the agencies they held contracts with. He had opened a Pandora's Box but didn't know it. When the COG and AAA Directors learned of his actions, they were livid. They knew they had to fight to regain control of the Waiver Program. One of the COG Executives initiated the fight by publicly accusing the State Welfare Commissioner of misleading Commissioner Rucker into giving up the waiver program. Commissioner Nelson, of the State Welfare Department, then went public, responding to the accusations, stating that he was trying to help Commissioner Rucker. When the Jefferson County AAA Director read what he had told the news reporters, she went after him with the media behind her.

When watching her on television news or reading an article in the newspaper, about an interview she had given, what you saw was a charming female. But knowing her as many across the state did, you knew that her charm was part of her fighting armor. She was known for her ability to fight you with a smile.

The other AAA Directors got the waiver clients and family members to call the state Welfare Commissioner and voice their concerns. The AAAs always made sure that TV news cameras and newspaper reporters were in the homes of the elderly throughout the week. During the interviews with waiver clients and family members, the reporters learned that the actions taken by the State Welfare Commissioner had resulted in the clients 'going without needed services. Senior citizens in nutrition centers were also kept informed, and they too got involved in the fight, speaking out against the State Welfare Commissioner.

Whereas senior citizens fought openly, the COG and AAA Directors met behind closed doors to discuss the problem and develop a solution. After much discussion, they realized that they needed help from their state legislators. After coming to that awareness, they formed a statewide task force with several state legislators. The task force would meet in Montgomery at various locations and at unusual times to discuss the problem. Their objective was to come up with a solution to regain control of the waiver program.

The COGs and AAA Directors were getting up and driving to Montgomery during the early morning hours. Those who lived in counties farther away would stay in Montgomery overnight. To avoid being seen, some of the meetings were scheduled as early as 4:00 a.m. Angela lived 112 miles away; she would sometimes be on the highway as early as 2:30 a.m. after getting a phone call the night before telling her she needed to be in Montgomery at 4:00 a.m.

When the COG Executives got together, they would sit around and talk about the force they had behind them. During their talks, they wanted to ensure that each COG Executive and AAA Director understood the fight they were taking on to accomplish their mission. They understood that they would have to fight dirty, using deceptive strategies to regain control of the waiver program. When the task force came together, they would discuss tactics they could employ. After several meetings and a great deal of deliberating a feasible option was agreed on. They decided to rewrite sections of the state budget bill. The same bill that was being debated. The state legislators who were members of the task force were men skilled at writing bills with loopholes. After having decided to rewrite the section of the state budget they discussed how they would go about getting the job done. After several late-night meetings, they decided on a plan of action as to how they would implement their plan. Several days later, after having carried out their plan, they sat back and waited for the passing of the state budget. Each day the AAAs sat in the legislature chamber, waiting for a vote on the state budget bill.

As time passed, the question as to how the problem had come about was asked. The COG Executives believed it was necessary to have all the facts to prevent the problem from happening again. Knowing they could not obtain the information from Commissioner Rucker or Susan, they made an appointment to talk with the state budget director. During their meeting, they learned that the former COA Commissioner had squandered the state matching dollars, leaving them without adequate matching dollars to carry them through the third year. Rumors were spreading around the state that the former Commissioner had given the money to some of the Regional Planning Commissions to purchase new automobiles. However, the stories were never confirmed nor disputed; but it was apparent because most of the Regional Planning Commissions had a fleet of beautiful, fully loaded new automobiles.

In light of the fact two of the twelve COG Executives were new in their jobs, the other COG Executives decided to give them some background information. They informed them about former problems the regions had gone through due to the shady dealings of people in top positions.

One of those problems was with the State Medicaid Agency. The state agency had drawn down and issued Federal Medicaid dollars without putting in the state matching portion. The federal government required the state to make a non-federal match for the money they gave for clients' services. In other words, for services costing $100.00, the state had to put in their matching portion, which was $27.00. That would have resulted in the federal government paying $73.00. But the state failed to put up its matching portion. This resulted in the cost of care being paid in full by the Federal Medicaid Agency. During a federal audit, the problem was discovered. The discrepancy over several years had resulted in Alabama owing the Federal Government millions of dollars. The State Medicaid Agency attempted to get out of paying the money back; they even got the clients and the clients' family members to write letters to the Federal Government asking the government to continue giving the state money, but the Federal Government refused. As months passed, the State Welfare Department and the Commission on Aging clients were going without needed services. After clients, family members and other officials put enough pressure on the state, the state paid the federal government, and the services were reinstated.

As time went **on**, task force members watched the state legislators debating on the state budget bill. Task force members would sit in the chambers, watching and listening to what was happening. When task force members were not in the voting chamber, they walked the halls talking to their representatives. When asked why they were spending so much time in Montgomery, they would tell the person(s) asking; that they were trying to learn the ways of politics. The fact was, they were keeping an eye on the three lines in the state budget bill that took away the State Welfare matching funds. The new wording put all of the matching dollars under the control of the 13-AAA.

The legislative members of the task force had gotten their secretaries to work with the COGs and AAAs to carry out an underhanded act. The secretaries went into the voting chambers and collected all the budget bills that had been left lying around. They had retyped the pages that showed the amount of state-matching dollars provided to the State Welfare Department. Without the matching funds, the State Welfare could not draw down any federal dollars. After changing the wording, they replaced the old pages with the newly typed pages and then shredded all the old pages.

As the debate on the state budget bill continued, the AAAs were in Montgomery daily. Cheryl, the Scott County Coordinator, would sometimes accompany Angela when their task force was not planning a night meeting. Angela and Cheryl would sit in the Legislature Chamber for hours, listening to the various debates.

One legislator filibustered for hours on the issue of putting stop signs on rural highways to protect the turtles as they made their way across county roads. He went further, suggesting that the state could build underground pathways so the turtles could travel from one side of the road to the other would be another option.

Each night after the legislators left, task force members would meet and review the entire budget to ensure their changes had not been discovered. After days had passed, the budget was finally voted on and approved. The AAA Directors then left the voting chamber but stayed in Montgomery. Later that night, after everyone had gone, task force members came together and reviewed the approved budget bill. Seeing that every word was still in place, they left and returned to their respective counties.

Chapter – Fifteen

MATCHING FUNDS TAKEN

One week after the state budget bill had been approved, the State Welfare Commissioner learned about the three lines in the budget that put the AAAs in charge of the matching dollars for the waiver program. Upon discovering the new wording and realizing that the State Welfare could not draw down federal Medicaid Waiver funds without going to the AAAs, Commissioner Nelson was beside himself with anger. Several individuals who spoke with the Commissioner said that it was evident that he was outdone. After he had calmed down, he realized that he had to bargain with the COGs and AAA Directors to recover his state matching funds.

To start the bargaining process, he invited all the COG Executives and AAA Directors to join the department staff for a lunch meeting. On the day of the meeting, he had a catering service put on an impressive luncheon. State Welfare Executives from the sixty-seven (67) counties were in attendance. Also, attending the meeting were news reporters and commissioners from the other state cabinets who benefited from the waiver program takeover. Commissioner Nelson made sure that each table had at least four of the county welfare executives sitting with the

COG and AAA Directors. Before getting down to business, they socialized, getting to know each other. Commissioner Nelson mingled in the crowd making sure the atmosphere was very pleasant. He shook hands with each of the AAA Directors and COG Executives. Earlier, when he had taken control of the Waiver Program, he had bragged, saying his cabinet was better qualified to manage the entire waiver program. He openly stated that the COGs and AAAs should never have been involved in providing the services. But the tables had turned, the COG Executives and AAA Directors were now holding the trump cards, and they had decided which hands to play.

When the meeting got started, Commissioner Nelson, first welcomed the group. Angela was seated next to one of her colleagues, as they watched him move about as he talked, Angela's colleague whispered, "*So that's what he looks like in person. He's an attractive, cute little fat fellow?*"

"*If you say so,*" Angela whispered.

Her colleague went on to say that several people had described him to her, but they had failed to tell her that he was cute. She then asked Angela if she had ever met him in person.

"*Yes, we've talked several times,*" Angela commented.

"*When, and about what?*"

"*When I was here turning in grant proposals,*" Angela said.

"*What kind of grants?*"

"*I administer several contracts for them*" Angela whispered. "*I'll tell you more when the meeting is over.*"

The two stopped whispering and started paying attention to what the Commissioner was saying.

"*I'm glad we could all come together to discuss the problem. Regrettably, we are here to solve a problem that never should have come about.*"

He then went on to explain a few things, stating that the AAAs primarily served older citizens, and his department served all age levels. As he spoke, the COG Executives and AAA Directors listened cautiously. During his speech, he came to a point where he made an effort to defend himself, saying that he was trying to be helpful and that his actions had been misconstrued. He began to pick up copies of newspapers and read the editorial columns. He stated that the articles written were misleading and said unkind things about him.

One of the COG Executives spoke out, telling him that they wanted to stick to the business they were there for and not waste time laying blame.

The Commissioner continued speaking telling the group that he never intended to take the Medicaid Waiver Program from COA. He then accused the COA staff of misappropriating the funds that created the problem. At that point, another COG Executive interrupted and informed him that the purpose of the meeting was to solve a problem and not cast blame. His statement opened the door for a prolonged discussion between several COG Executives, AAA Directors, and Commissioner Nelson.

Ms. Henderson then spoke out asking Commissioner Nelson, what made him think that the county welfare agencies could take on the responsibility of serving all the state's homebound elderly. Commissioner Nelson then told the attendees that he had a department in every county, and they were capable of serving all the elderly clients. The discussion continued with Commissioner Nelson bringing up some of the allegations that had been written in the newspaper. One of the AAA Directors spoke out, saying that his agency had gotten hundreds of calls from family members asking why their mother, father, or other elderly relatives were no longer receiving services. He went on to say that everything was going fine until Commissioner Nelson took control of the entire Waiver Program *"Now..., that's one of the misunderstandings. I didn't take the program; Commissioner Rucker gave it to me."*

Commissioner Nelson went on to say that he had been told that the former COA Commissioner had squandered all of COA matching state funds and given the COGs a fleet of new automobiles. The COA Executives who had not benefitted began speaking out saying, *"I didn't benefit no one gave my agency a fleet of new automobiles."*

The discussion as to which COGs had benefitted went on for a while before they returned to the issue they were all there for. After his statement, many unnecessary accusations were thrown into the discussion.

Commissioner Nelson stated that he was a fair and decent man and would never stoop so low as to deceive another cabinet member into giving up a program. But the COGs and AAAs were so stirred up that his statements trying to justify his actions meant nothing. Finally, after a considerable amount of time had been spent debating and they had not been able to solve the problem, the meeting was adjourned.

The task force members then gathered in another conference room to discuss the outcome. Several COG Executives expressed their displeasure regarding some of the harsh things Ms. Henderson had said to Commissioner Nelson. In her defense, she explained that if the task force didn't put pressure on Commissioner Nelson, he would think he had the power to take control of the waiver program again. With her comment, the group realized they couldn't take a chance and let him assume they would not fight back.

Two weeks later, after many phone calls, the COG and AAA Directors decided to go back to Montgomery and work out a solution. The second meeting was much smaller, without all the fanfare of the first meeting. The accusations that had been made and the hurt feelings were set aside. Finally, after much debating, the groups came to a resolution, and the battle to regain the Medicaid Waiver Program was resolved. After working out some issues, the COG Executives and AAA Directors met with Commissioner Rucker to return the Waiver Program's management to COA.

Back home in the thirteen regions, the newspaper reporters wrote articles about the fierce battle between the State Welfare Commissioner, the Council of Governments Executives, and the Area Agency on Aging Directors. The newspapers reported that the fight was initiated when one of the AAA criticized the State Welfare Commissioner for taking the Waiver Program.

For twelve of the thirteen AAA Directors, their fight was over. However, for Angela, a new battle was about to begin. In addition to her full-time job as AAA Director, Angela served on several boards. One of those boards was the 'Ms. Senior Alabama Pageant'.

Angela was put in a position of having to deal with a problem that was developing on the Ms. Senior Alabama Pageant board. She served as the Assistant State Pageant Director for the 'Ms. Senior Alabama Pageant'. The state director was Ms. Sally Snow. Sally had formed the pageant in 1985. Alabama was the 23rd State to Incorporate and create a senior beauty pageant. Two years prior, in 1987, Ms. Gilda Campbell from Auburn, AL, won the state title of *"Ms. Senior Alabama."*

The board was then responsible for sending Gilda to Atlantic City to compete for the national title. At that time, the pageant did not have the support of the state, and they were struggling for financial support. During the early phase of the pageant, Angela, Charlotte, and Sally, who were board officers, supported the pageant using personal funds and the small amount of money they could raise or obtain from other board members. However, despite their financial shortfall, the pageant sent its state winner and the state director to Atlantic City in 1988 to compete. In the competition, Gilda put on a show that won her the national title of 'Ms. Senior America'. After her achievement, the pageant gained statewide recognition and state financial support. The board then paid Angela the $900.00 she had loaned the pageant, which had enabled the state winner and state director to attend the national competition. Her contributions to helping the pageant gain recognition were honored with an appreciation plaque.

Around early November 1989, when everything seemed to have been going well, Craig, one of the pageant board members, stopped by Angela's office. His visit was to solicit Angela's support in reorganizing the pageant board. He wanted board members to ask the state director to resign and appoint him to replace her. During his talk, he spoke of the financial problems the pageant had faced and the money Angela had loaned the pageant. He stated, *"Of course, you will get your money back when we reorganize and the board appoints me as state director."*

His statement surprised Angela, considering the board had already paid her the $900.00. As he continued talking, she sat quietly listening, waiting to hear how he planned to have Sally removed from her position. As he laid out his plan for managing the pageant, Angela interrupted and asked where he would get the money to implement all the planned changes. At that moment, Craig begins talking about the amount of money the pageant would be getting from the state and other supporting organizations. Hearing this, Angela realized that Craig did not understand how much they had put into putting on the pageants. In addition to the money Angela loaned the pageant, she contributed by having her aging program secretary perform all the typing. The Commission had made many contributions: The pageant's printing of handouts, brochures, and mail-outs was done at no expense to the pageant. Angela and other board members had prepared the food and beverages for all of their pageant meetings and the competition recital. After Gilda had become *MS Senior America*, Angela sponsored a large reception with a layout of foods and beverages.

After Craig talked for more than an hour without being challenged about his plan, he thought he had gained Angela's support.

Immediately after he left, Angela called Sally and Charlotte. She informed them of Craig's intent to make a motion to dismiss Sally as state director and have one of his supporters make a motion to have him take over. Sally then called Nella, a retired attorney who served on the pageant board, and told Nella about Craig's intent. Later that week, several trusted board members met and devised a plan to prevent Craig's scheme from gaining ground. To better understand how many board members supported Craig, Charlotte, and Angela called each member for a friendly chat. They wanted to know the number of board members who favored seeing Sally step down.

Several weeks later, at the pageant's board meeting, Craig entered the room feeling confident he would be the next state pageant director. All board members were present for the first time in several months. The meeting was called to order, and everything was carried out according to the Robert Rules of Orders. But Sally, being in a rush to find out what Craig's plans were, quickly went through the general program business, then asked for new business. At that moment, Craig stood and presented his case, then asked for a motion to have the state director step down. A motion was made and seconded by two of Craig's four supporters. Sally's removal was then put on the table for discussion. After much discussion, the Robert Rules of Order were disregarded when the discussion got out of hand. Charlotte started confronting Craig about his failure to financially support Gilda's trip to Atlantic City. She then told Craig that the board was no longer in need of his services, considering he hadn't done much to support the pageant. Charlotte then looked at board members seated around the large table and asked for a motion to have Craig, and his supporters dismissed as board members. A motion was quickly given and seconded. At that moment, Sally's supporters all stood in unity. Craig and his supporters were then told to leave. The expressions on their faces, as they were getting up to leave, showed that they were stunned.

After the meeting adjourned, Angela and Charlotte walked to their cars, discussing what had occurred. They both agreed that Craig had to be a fool to think that Angela would vote to dismiss Sally and make a motion nominating him to replace Sally. They then started talking about the Atlantic City trip.

"Did I tell you he wanted to go to Atlantic City and be recognized as a state board member?" Angela asked.

"No, you didn't, but I knew he wanted to go."

"I told him it would be a nice gesture, but he would have to pay his expense," Angela said.

"So that's why he didn't go."

"Yes, that was the reason. He had thought that the board would pay for his expense," Angela said with a chuckle.

After they had laughed and talked about Craig, Charlotte changed the subject and started inquiring about Angela's job. She wanted to know how things were going with Camilla and Lynette.

"You don't want to know," Angela told her.

"Yes, I do."

Considering Angela and Charlotte were close friends who often used each other as a sounding board, Angela decided to tell Charlotte what was happening. She told Charlotte about the budget-overspending plot Camilla had set in motion, then took off on leave. She went on to say that Camilla and Lynette were hoping that she wouldn't discover the problem before it got out of control.

"Angela, how did you find out about the overspending?"

"Judy the accountant brought it to my attention."

"When you say overspending, how much damage was done?" Charlotte asked.

"It was approaching $80K."

"Shit! That was a lot of money,"

"Yes, it was."

Angela went on to say that after she had gotten over the shock, she went into action making a lot of changes.

"What type of changes?"

As Charlotte listened Angela told her about the many changes she had made, and how Camilla and Lynette had reacted.

"Girl…, you should have fired them."

"I wish I could have, but Mr. Percy wouldn't allow it."

Angela went on to say that working with Camilla and Lynette was like working with Satan himself.

"Your biggest problem is your boss," Charlotte said.

Angela let out a short chuckle; *"You're right, but I'm okay because I know that God's got my back."*

Angela then quoted *Proverbs 18:10. The name of the LORD is a strong tower the righteous run to it and are safe.*

Chapter – Sixteen

LIES AND PROMISES

Angela went on to tell Charlotte, that Mr. Percy believes Camilla would eventually change and accept the fact that the executive committee thought she would be the better choice for that position.

"I don't believe either of those women will ever come to that conclusion," Charlotte said with a giggle.

Angela agreed saying she didn't foresee them accepting that fact.

"Well, seems like you are handling the problems."

"I am, but I must admit I don't think I could if I didn't believe in the words written in Roman 8:28."

"What does that scripture say?"

"If you believe and trust God, He will work all things out for your good, and I believe that things will turn out according to His plan."

"Girl…, you sound like a preacher."

Angela then chuckled, *"Oh well,"* she commented.

"I'm sorry they're giving you so much trouble," Charlotte said.

"Believe it, I'm going to be okay."

Angela went on to say that each day before going to work, she would spiritually equip herself for the battle she knew she had to fight.

Charlotte then took out a pen and piece of paper and asked Angela to give her some scriptures she could read.

"Why? Just study your Bible. Angela said as she began citing several books she enjoyed reading. They were the Psalms, Proverbs, Ephesians, Roman and Ecclesiastes."

"You stay so positive despite all the mess you have to deal with. Maybe, if I read the Bible more often it will help me put up with my boss."

Charlotte went on to say that working with the mayor was the same as working with Ms. Henderson.

"You don't say," Angela said with a giggle.

After talking for a while longer, they departed.

Charlotte was an attractive light-complex female with red shoulder-length hair. She was approximately 5'7" tall, with her weight in proportion to her height.

As Angela was driving back to the office, she wondered what Camilla and Lynette could be up to. They had openly apologized and re-established their relationships with most of the staff. Things were truly going well, or so it appeared. However, the division directors had reservations about Camilla and Lynette's modified behavior and warned Angela not to let her guard down. During a conversation Angela had with Blair, she told him that Camilla and Lynette were so friendly it made her want to throw up. She told him that their changed behavior convinced her that they were up to no good.

As weeks passed, having regained control of the Medicaid Waiver Program; gotten spending back in line, and gotten rid of the problem on the beauty pageant board, Angela had more time to deal with in-house aging issues. As she was going through some documents that had been mounting up, she looked at Camilla and Lynette's leave forms and saw that they had been taking time off on the same days. One would take a vacation day and the other one would call in sick.

Later that day, during a conversation Angela had with Valeria, Angela learned that Commissioner James had asked Valeria why Camilla and Lynette were spending so much time in Clair County with Susan. Knowing they had no reason for traveling around with Susan during work hours, Angela and Valeria decided to call around to find out if they had been seen together in other counties. After speaking with several people in different counties, they learned that Susan, Councilwoman Jones, Lynette, and Camilla had met with the mayors of several small towns in their region. With this information, Angela began to pay closer attention to their time off.

When Angela told Mr. Percy about what she was learning, he brushed her off by telling her that he didn't believe they would do such. He would end the conversation by telling her to get off of their backs and try to work with them. He was unyielding in his belief about their trustworthiness. They had him convinced, that they were loyal to the Planning Commission. They would flatter him every chance they got to keep him thinking that he could trust them. Angela, believing she knew what they were up to and did not have the support or power to do anything about it, began keeping everything to herself.

As time passed, knowing that she could not discuss the problems with Mr. Percy, Angela felt like she was fighting a battle with no recourse. Those feelings lead to stress-related health issues. When she went to the doctor for a check-up, the doctor could not find any medical issues that were causing the problems so he prescribed medication to help her overcome the stress. Being a woman of strong Christian faith and having been told by her doctor that he saw no reason for her health problems, she chose not to take the medications but instead demonstrated that she was trusting in the word of God. She continued reading daily scriptures to reinforce her faith in the word of God.

Romans 8, 'for we know that all things work together for good to those who love God, to those who are the called according to His purpose.'

Believing firmly in those words kept her going. She truly believed that everything would work out for her good. Reading certain scriptures kept her spiritually equipped with the confidence and strength she needed for the battle.

As weeks went by, Susan and Councilwoman Jones would travel through the region to build a greater team of supporters. At some point, Susan gained the support of three Scott County Republican County

Commissioners. The three county commissioners were grasping for power and name recognition. Given their time in office, they had created many problems fighting with their democratic counterpart. With the three now on board, Susan and Councilwoman Jones believed they now had sufficient power to take the aging program.

Since the election of Governor Hanson, the three Scott County Republican Commissioners would travel throughout Scott County trying to persuade other citizens to switch over to the Republican Party. During their presentations, they talked a lot about Jefferson County and how Jefferson County was growing by taking possession of unincorporated sub-divisions in Scott County. They promised the citizens great things stating they could bring jobs and businesses to the county. They pointed out that the only way they could accomplish that would be to compete with Birmingham. They asked the citizens to get on board and help them go after state-funded programs that had their main office located in Birmingham. One of the programs was the aging program. They promised the citizens that the aging program would create jobs and bring millions of dollars to Scott County. That promise was very encouraging to hear, and the citizens were jumping on board. Feeling confident they were gaining ground, Susan, Councilwoman Jones, and several others formed a team and referred to it as the pull-out team. Team members would travel throughout the five-county region, telling the citizens that the party's growth guaranteed them help from the governor.

While Susan was in the field gaining support, COA learned that the extra federal funds they had previously been able to acquire were dwindling, so COA prepared letters to send to the AAAs. Susan took the letter addressed to the Planning Commission and held on to it. This allowed her to promote her agenda by distorting the information written in the letter. She would take the letter with her when the group met with members of the county aging program boards and other interested county and city officials. Susan would read sections of the letter that got their attention. She would then follow up by talking about things not written in the letter. Her strategy was to give the impression that the Planning Commission was getting a significant cut in funding, which would result in the Planning Commission having to make cuts in the budgets of the county aging programs. She would tell them that the cuts would not be necessary if the Planning Commission would reduce the in-direct cost they were charging the aging program. Hearing about the cuts and the in-direct cost was disturbing to county residents, and they wanted to know if there was a way to prevent the county programs from getting the cuts. Susan informed them that the only way to offset the shortfalls in funding would be to take the aging program from under the Planning Commission and set it up as an independent entity. She led them to believe that action would drastically reduce the overhead and administrative costs of operating the aging program. Susan went so far as to prepare an organizational chart showing the counties how much they would gain by pulling from under the Planning Commission. Seeing the increase of $150,000 annually, many people who heard the presentations believed the information; especially with it coming from the COA Deputy Director.

Several days after the pull-out team members had met with Clair County officials, Angela received a telephone call from Clara. Clara told her that she had some important documents she wanted Angela to see. Angela, thinking the information could be faxed, asked Enda to fax the documents; but Clara declined for fear the documents could end up in Camilla's hand. Wanting to see the information, Angela drove the 42 miles to meet with Clara. When she arrived, she was surprised to see County Commissioner Elmore and the aging program board chairman. After chatting for a short time, they began explaining the reason for the meeting. They told Angela about the information Susan had presented at various meetings. They then asked Angela to tell them how she was going to handle the problem. Angela explained that she had recently gotten a letter from COA stating that the additional funds they had previously been able to draw down were dwindling. She explained that this was due to a decrease in federal funds, which COA had been able to obtain by writing grants. She then explained that the shortfalls in funding would not affect the county's aging programs because she did not lose any of her level of funding. Angela went on to commend Clara for writing grants to obtain different funds. Listening to Angela's explanations the three appeared satisfied, however, they believed that Mr. Percy needed to confront Susan about the rumors she was spreading. Considering, the pull-out team had not yet persuaded the heads of the four counties to pull away, Commissioner Elmore told Angela that he would talk to Mr. Percy about his failure to speak out. After further discussion, the two men left. Watching them drive away Clara took out copies of the information she wanted Angela to read. As Angela looked at the organization charts and the budget sheets, she was amazed. The charts showed that Camilla would be the AAA Director, with Cheryl, Scott County Aging Program Coordinator as her assistant. Lynette would become the nutrition services coordinator, and Councilwoman Jones would be the executive director of a new agency they would establish. On the organization board they would form, would be all the republican county commissioners. Other positions the organization would need were written in with a notation that the position would be filled later. This information had not impressed Clara, for they failed to show how she would benefit from the move other than promising that Clair County would get an additional $150,000 annually. Enda's thought of getting more money was great but knowing that she would have to deal with the new management team turned Clara off. Clara told Angela that they had been assured that things would be done differently under the new organization, but they had failed to explain what they meant.

After Angela and Clara had chatted for a while longer, Clara made copies of the information sheets and gave them to Angela, with a promise from Angela that she would not reveal where she had gotten the copies from.

As Angela drove back to her office, she was confident this information would get Mr. Percy's attention. She felt sure he would want to look into the matter and take action.

Chapter – Seventeen

OTHER ISSUES

When she returned she went straight to Mr. Percy's office and showed him the information. But as always, he was confident that they could not take the program. He was sure the Planning Commission Executive Committee would have called and told him if anything was going on. He attempted to ease Angela's mind by telling her about earlier pull-out attempts. He told her every detail that had taken place years earlier. Many of the exact details she had already heard about. As he talked, Angela sat and listened but said nothing. When she thought he had finished, she got up and started walking toward the door, but he started talking again no sooner than she had opened the door.

"I tell you, my board will not allow them to take the program," he said.

Angela turned and said, *"Mr. Percy, Susan's new position gives her a little more clout. The executive committee may not be able to prevent it."*

"Again…, I say it will never happen. My executive committee will not allow it."

During the next two weeks, Clara and her board chairman called Angela three to four times each week to find out if Mr. Percy was going to say anything. They wanted him to dispute the financial information Susan was passing out, but he refused.

As weeks passed and the talk about pulling the program ceased, Mr. Percy felt confident that he was right. He would stop by Angela's office, nod, and say, *"I told you so."*

Unfortunately, he was not alone in his thinking. Many others were thinking the same way, but they were all wrong. The pull-out team had not given up; the problem was some of the more influential team members were fighting other battles.

Scott County was rapidly growing and dealing with development problems during that time. One of their main problems was the City of Birmingham was also growing, annexing unincorporated communities in Scott County. These communities had the homes of Scott County's more affluent citizens who needed services that Scott County could not provide. Seeing the opportunity to develop southward, Birmingham's mayor took advantage of Scott County's slow development problems. The mayor frequently met with citizens in Scott County who were trying to acquire services their subdivisions needed. These services could only be obtained if they were annexed into a city, and Birmingham was willing to take them in and give them what they needed. When the citizens voted to annex, Birmingham came through; the Birmingham mayor immediately gave them the services.

All of the service providers would be parked along the road waiting for the mayor's call. When the call came, the wheels would start rolling; fire trucks, paramedics, and police cars were parked on the sites of the newly annexed property within minutes. A large sign was immediately put up, showing all the services the newly annexed communities would get. A large picture of a fire department with fire trucks and paramedics standing by the vehicles was displayed in the annexed area. A billboard along the main highway would show that Birmingham had annexed the property. At the subdivision entrance, emergency vehicles, patio tables, chairs with a huge umbrella, and an outdoor latrine were put in place for the service providers.

Birmingham displays created major traffic jams down Highway

280, with drivers taking pictures and residents driving by to see their new service providers. Men and women providing the services waved as cars passed. It was indeed a sight you wouldn't want to miss. It was like a parade, with the main attraction turning the corner and the viewers yelling when they saw the first line. The car horns would blow, and the people would yell: "*Thank you, Birmingham!*"

Scott County officials were outraged seeing Birmingham annexing these large subdivisions that had homes of Scott County's wealthier citizens. To demonstrate their anger, they would go to the Republican Governor and ask him to relocate the main office of state programs to Scott County. They had voted for Governor Hanson, and he was paying them back with political favors.

Each time Birmingham annexed communities in Scott County, the fight between the Mayor of Birmingham and Scott County Officials became more hostile. One would only need to attend a Scott County Commissioners meeting, read the newspaper, and follow up with a drive down Highway 280 to understand what was causing the hostility. You could go in and out of Birmingham during the drive, and that made Birmingham Scott County's worst enemy.

Scott County officials fought Birmingham on every issue, big or small. Scott County's newspaper reported that Birmingham had stolen a broom from Scott County waterworks. A week later, the newspaper reported that Scott County officials were filing a lawsuit against Talladega County for selling water rights to Jefferson County for the communities in Scott County Birmingham had annexed.

To know who the target was on any given day, one would only have to read the Birmingham newspaper or the Scott County Reporter.

The Planning Commission Division Directors traveled around the region and spoke with the county and city officials informing them of the services the Commission offered. Three of the Commission's Division Directors had gone to Scott County to speak at a County Commissioner's meeting. Angela, one of the three, sat observing the county commissioners while her two colleagues, Jerry and Blair, gave their presentations. It was noticeable that the three Republican county commissioners had already decided to attack the three, and were simply waiting for the opportunity. During Blair's presentation, they criticized everything he said. The Commissioners made it clear that Scott County wanted its fair share of the federal transportation money even after being told that the federal dollars were used for Interstates. The three County Commissioners responded as little kids. During Blair's presentation, they frequently asked why they couldn't form their county planning commission and get their own money. When Blair would attempt to explain how the state was divided into regional planning districts, they would interrupt him and say: *"We know that, but the state now has a Republican Governor, and he will work with us."*

From the attitude displayed by the three Republican County Commissioners, Angela realized that she was in for a thorough interrogation. When the time finally arose for Angela to give her presentation, she stepped up to the podium. Commissioner Hudson snickered, turned to his colleagues, and whispered something, but Angela did not allow his snickering to bother her; she confidently presented her report. Immediately after she had finished speaking, the attack was on. Commissioner Hudson asked the questions and his colleagues sat listening and staring at Angela. One of his colleagues nodded on several occasions giving the impression that he was satisfied with Angela's answers, but the other Commissioner, like Commissioner Hudson, seemed unwilling to accept any answers. The two only wanted an explanation as to why Scott County was a part of the Regional Planning Commission and why the Commission was telling them what to do. As they questioned Angela, she stood like a proud Marine and took the heat.

After the Planning Commission presenters had finished their presentations, they decided to stay and see how the other presenters would be treated. To their amazement, they saw that the other presenters were treated the same as they had been treated. The only difference they noticed was when the presenters introduced themselves as fellow Republicans; then they were treated more respectfully.

Among the many problems Scott County Commissioners were dealing with; they were slow in establishing zoning ordinances. This created significant problems in their development. At commissioners' meetings, citizens frequently complained about issues dealing with the development of schools, shopping centers, fire stations, and police departments, residential and grazing land. One could drive through some areas and see lovely homes surrounded by pastures of livestock. During certain seasons of the year, the homeowners had to go past a field of foul-smelling animal manure.

In addition to the complaints from the residents, the county commissioners were fighting amongst themselves. Their fights were always between three of their four Republican Commissioners and their only Democratic Commissioner.

The major problem was, that Commissioner Hudson wanted the job held by Commissioner Miller, a Democrat, and the county probate judge. Commissioner Miller had held his position for more than twelve years. Commissioner Hudson wanted the role so desperately he would spare no one the heat of his rage to obtain it. Being a longtime resident of the southern part of Scott County, Commissioner Miller had the support of those residents. He was also likable, much more so than his Republican counterparts. People always referred to him as a good old Southern gentleman. In comparison, Commissioner Hudson was seen as a man grasping for power.

Commissioner Miller was a good-looking, White male with a friendly, pleasant facial expression. He appeared to be in his early fifties. He stood approximately 6'4", with his weight in proportion to his height. He had honey-blond hair, which he wore neatly cut and trimmed.

Commissioner Hudson was also a nice-looking White male, about the age of forty-eight. His weight was well in proportion to his 5'11" stature. He was always well-dressed, wearing a three-piece dark pin-stripe suit.

In addition to the other problems the county had to deal with, their Republican County Commissioners had come into office with the goal of unseating Commissioner Miller. Commissioner Hudson was a progressive Republican who would go to any extreme to succeed and get his name and picture in the newspaper. He jumped on every bandwagon to gain media attention. His supporters, two Republican County Commissioners who had come into office during the same period him, were always preaching a sermon of wanting to move Scott County ahead. They believed the best way to accomplish that goal was to get more support from voters. They were always meeting with groups of citizens around the county encouraging them to switch their party affiliation. It was apparent their message was catching on. Many county residents were jumping on the bandwagon and switching their party alliances.

Weekly, newspaper headlines would feature citizens who had switched parties. The headlines would read: 'Mr. & Mrs. John Acorn switched political parties.' A picture of the people would be shown, and an article would explain their rationale for switching parties. Sometimes the people who had switched parties were displayed together like characters from the movie, 'The Beverly Hillbillies.' Unfortunately, they did not have Jed Clampett's wealth. Their comments would always begin with: 'We were Democrats all our lives, but we are now proud to say we pledge our allegiance to the Republican Party.'

Another problem Scott County had was Commissioner Hudson and his two counterparts always played dirty underhanded politics, trying to get the upper hand on Commissioner Miller. They created jobs and hired their friends despite the opposition of Commissioner Miller and the other county commissioner, who was a Republican.

Commissioner Miller had many responsibilities; among them was signing off on the hiring and other personnel-related issues. To keep up with Commissioner Miller, the Republican County Commissioners decided to hire Jason Blevins as his administrative assistant. Commissioner Miller believed that Commissioner Hudson and his counterparts were trying to put Jason in a position so they could spy on him. Believing as he did, Commissioner Miller refused to sign off on anything relating to Jason. Despite his refusal, the Republican Commissioners assigned a workplace for Jason. The only thing in his workplace was a desk and a chair. Daily, Jason would frivolously sit at his desk, doing absolutely nothing, while Commissioner Miller went about his duties, paying no attention to Jason.

Weekly newspaper reporters would stop in and take pictures of Jason. Seeing Jason sitting there doing nothing was hilarious. For Jason's 44th birthday, one of the commissioners' secretaries gave him a yellow toy telephone. Seeing the pictures the photojournalist had captured of Jason holding the toy phone to his ear and mouth had the citizens around the region laughing and joking about the situation.

Commissioner Miller's refusal to sign off on Jason's hiring resulted in the Republican Commissioners filing a lawsuit against Commissioner Miller. While the suit was going on, Commissioner Hudson got Jason involved in their fight to take the aging program from the Planning Commission. Being enthusiastic about his assignment, Jason immediately scheduled a meeting with Mr. Percy to come in and discuss the aging program issues. During the meeting, Mr. Percy provided Jason with a great deal of information. As Mr. Percy talked, Jason pretended to be taking down all the information; he even assured Mr. Percy that he would go back and report all the facts. After their meeting, Mr. Percy showed Jason around the agency and introduced him to the staff. After Jason had left, Mr. Percy joyfully walked around, assuring the staff that Jason was there to obtain factual information to take back to the county commissioners.

Chapter – Eighteen

EFFORTS INCREASE

H ours later, the TV news reporters were giving highlights of the upcoming evening news. It was reported that no sooner than Jason had gotten back to Scott County, he called and set up meetings with all the surrounding news media. When Mr. Percy learned about the upcoming news report of his discussion with Jason he was very excited. He could hardly wait to hear what Jason had told them. Later that evening, when the news came on, Mr. Percy learned that Jason had told the reporters many lies. Jason informed the reporters of his meeting with Mr. Percy, stating he understood why Scott County wanted to pull the aging program from under the Planning Commission management. He criticized the Commission's in-direct cost and the amount of money the aging program paid, to be a part of the Commission. He complained about the Commission staff's large salaries and told the reporters that the county's aging programs would greatly benefit if pulled from under the Commission. The reporters informed the viewers they would be providing additional information after they had an opportunity to speak with Mr. Percy.

The following morning, the reporters showed up at the Commission to get Mr. Percy's response to Jason's allegations. From their questions, you could hear Mr. Percy yell as he attempted to clarify what he had told Jason. He told the reporters he had no idea where Jason had gotten the information he had given to them. Immediately after the reporters left, Mr. Percy called Jason. Jason was waiting and ready to talk; Jason denied reporting the information presented in the news. He convinced Mr. Percy that the only way to resolve the discrepancies in what was said was for him to come back for more talks. The Commission's staff was furious that Mr. Percy was giving in to Jason and allowing him to return. They could see that Jason was playing Mr. Percy for a fool and taking advantage of Mr. Percy's trusting nature.

The following day when Jason arrived, only the executive secretary and one of the receptionists were present. All the staff had signed out to various locations, so they wouldn't have to see Jason. Later that evening, after being told by the executive secretary how Jason had beguiled Mr. Percy with flattering remarks, the Commission staff had little to no respect for Jason.

Reading the newspaper and listening to the news about the lawsuit that was going on about the hiring of Jason, the Planning Commission staff was rejoicing, hoping that Commissioner Miller would win the case so that he could get rid of Jason. Jason had joined the fight to take the aging program and had become one of the Commission's enemies.

As Commissioner Hudson's proxy, Jason would attend the Planning Commission Executive Committee meetings with Councilwoman Jones. The two were highly opinionated; they criticized everything said about the success and accomplishments of the aging programs. Many individuals who attended the meetings asked why the Commission would allow Jason and Councilwoman Jones to express their negative opinions, and not publicly respond to the negative allegations. One of the attendees was overheard telling several others that Jason was taking advantage of an opportunity to speak out, considering he was never allowed to say anything at the Scott County Commissioners' meetings.

Several months later, after attending a Scott County Commissioners' night meeting, Jason was involved in an automobile accident. The following day news reported that Jason had driven off the road and was taken to the hospital. When the Commission staff read the newspaper, they joyfully cheered. Two of the staff members were standing in the reception area reading the newspaper and talking about Jason and the accident;

One said to the other, *"I hope the accident teaches him a lesson."*

"Yes, I hope so. He could have been killed."

"I hate to admit it, but I wouldn't be sorry," one of the two said.

"I can imagine Commissioner Miller would agree with you." The other one stated.

The secretary who heard the conversation thought nothing much of the comments, for she knew that most of the staff would probably agree with the two. For they were outraged with Jason because of the lies he had been telling.

Later that afternoon, when more details about the accident were given, it was reported that Jason's condition was critical.

"I can imagine he is lying there thinking about his lies." The receptionist said to the secretary.

After hearing more details about Jason's injuries, the staff did not abstain from making negative comments. The majority of them continued expressing unkind things about him. The following day news report stated that his condition had worsened, and his doctor had said it would be a miracle if he pulled through.

As the receptionist was reading the newspaper, Shelley, one of the aging program staff members, walked past her desk.

"Have you read the morning newspaper?" The receptionist asked.

"Why? Is Jason dead yet?" Shelley asked.

"No, he's still hanging on."

"Oh well," Shelley said as she continued on her way.

Each time an updated report about Jason's health was announced, a few staff members continued making unsympathetic statements about him.

During Jason's hospitalization, his wife entered the battle and filed a lawsuit against Scott County Commissioners, seeking medical coverage and unpaid wages. Several weeks later, Jason died.

After hearing the report of his death, the Commission staff was stunned and made no further comments.

During Jason's months of involvement in the fight to take the aging program, he played a significant role in keeping everything stirred up. There was hardly a day that went by without Jason speaking to reporters and saying negative things about the Planning Commission.

As time passed, the energy behind the fight to take the program appeared to have been dropped. Unfortunately, that was not the case, the problem was several of the individuals who were involved in the fight were busy dealing with other more important issues. Susan was sometimes engaged in job-related duties that kept her occupied. The Scott County Commissioners' ongoing fights among themselves kept them busy with little or no time to go outside the county to stir up problems.

However, the team members' temporary lack of involvement didn't stop Camilla and Lynette. They were busy engaging in tactics trying to sway the in-house staff into believing they were fully committed to supporting the Commission, but the only person who was being misled was Mr. Percy. He was sure they were not involved in the plot to take the aging program. Fortunately, Angela was not being misled. She was convinced that Camilla, Lynette, Susan, and Councilwoman Jones were still engaged in developing a plan to take the program. One of the things that kept Angela alert was Camilla and Lynette's actions after taking a day or two off. They would come back to work overflowing with enthusiasm and reaching out to give everybody a helpful hand at whatever they were doing.

During that time, Susan and Councilwoman Jones were traveling around the region, telling everyone who would listen to them about Susan's problems while employed with the Commission. Susan lied and said she had to pay the Commission a large portion of the aging program funding to cover the indirect cost. Her main objective was to ruin the Commission's reputation by giving the small-town officials the impression that the Commission was misappropriating federal money.

Many of the people she spoke with believed her because of their lack of understanding of the in-direct and shared cost concepts. However, when she spoke to more affluent groups of individuals, and one of them asked for more information or clarification, she could not give an intelligent answer.

As time passed, Susan began to gain more supporters after Mr. Percy continued his refusal to respond to the lies she was spreading. Believing that maybe she was being truthful, the Clair County Republican Commissioners decided to unite with Scott County Commissioners. Several weeks later, they were able to talk Cook County Republican Commissioners into joining their effort. After the three counties came together, they decided to get the media involved. The reporters would unexpectedly visit the counties and speak with the county coordinators. When they visited Clair County, Clara told them that the Planning Commission took in hundreds of thousands of dollars in federal monies and other allocations and gave the money out as administrative outlays to the thirteen area agencies. Even though Clara was a great county co-ordinator with a great program, her statement sounded like something a dumb person would say. People in the aging network who read the newspaper laughed because her statement gave the Planning Commission more power and reduced the function of the State Commission on Aging.

With all the misleading information being spread around, Mr. Percy took no action. He always said he would not lower himself to respond to negative comments. COG Executives from around the state talked to him daily, encouraging him to speak out and dispute Susan's lies. They tried to convince him that his failure to speak out would result in people believing what they were reading or being told. Unfortunately, his failure to depute the lies Susan was telling had many readers believing her.

When Angela spoke with reporters, she would always give them factual information that contradicted what the opposing team had told them. She expected intelligent, educated individuals to understand, but still, they seemed more interested in publishing the lies they had been told by the opposing team members.

Chapter – Nineteen

THREE RESOLUTIONS

The Planning Commission's monthly Executive Committee meetings were generally attended only by Mr. Percy, his secretary, executive committee members, division directors, project heads, and a few other Commission members. However, with the ongoing talk of the three counties wanting to pull the aging services from under the Planning Commission, many people became interested in knowing what the outcome would be. As the plot to take the program progressed, more people would attend the meetings to see if anything would happen. The conference room would be crowded with reporters, opposing team members, and COG Executives from around the state. When the meetings ended without the opposing team members saying anything, many people started believing the effort to take the program had been abandoned, and they saw no reason to continue coming.

After several months had gone by the opposing team showed up at the Planning Commission's monthly executive committee meeting in record numbers. Several, commissioners who very rarely attended the meeting, but always sent in a proxy were present on that day. Seeing them conversing, Angela got a feeling that they were up to something.

Whereas the county commissioners would stop by the division director's office and chat for a few minutes, on that day, the opposing county commissioners had gone directly to the conference room.

As Jerry and Angela were headed to the conference room, they met Commissioner Hunt of Woodrow County. The three started chatting, for they still had twenty minutes before the meeting was to begin.

Commissioner Hunt then asked Jerry to excuse him while he and Angela talked. Commissioner Hunt told Angela that Mr. Percy had told several executive committee members that she believed Lynette and Camilla were working with Susan to take the aging program. He said that Mr. Percy was concerned because it was affecting her relationship with the two. He went on to say that he had promised Mr. Percy that he would talk to her. Listening to the things Commissioner Hunt was saying, Angela felt somewhat embarrassed. She then told him that she had been told that Lynette and Camilla were traveling around the region with Susan and Councilwoman Jones, who were trying to persuade county officials to pull from under the Planning Commission.

"That may be true, but Susan hasn't spoken to Woodrow County Commissioners," he said.

Thinking that they had finished their private conversation, Jerry returned. Jerry told Commissioner Hunt and Angela he was surprised to see several county commissioners who seldom attended the meetings. As Jerry talked, Commissioner Hunt's attention was drawn to a group of news reporters going into the conference room.

"What's on the agenda?" He asked. "Several reporters just went into the conference room."

"As I said moments ago, I see county commissioners who always send in a proxy," Jerry said.

Commissioner Hunt then said, "Maybe they're here to show their support for the Commission."

Angela didn't comment because she was thinking just the opposite. She then excused herself and returned to her office to get the documents she had planned to give to several executive committee members. However, in light of what Commissioner Hunt had just said, she had failed to mention the documents during their conversation. After getting the documents, she stopped at the receptionist's desk and gave her the folder, telling her that she may need to have copies made. As she was headed to the conference room, she saw Scott County Commissioner Hudson and several others, among them were Councilwoman Jones, and several individuals she didn't recognize. They were standing in the corner near the conference room talking. Her intuition led her to become better equipped for what may come about. She then went back to the receptionist and asked her to go ahead and make forty copies of the documents. As she was giving the receptionist instructions, Valeria walked up and asked if she needed help. Angela told Valeria that she might not need the documents but wanted to be prepared. She and Valeria then left, going to the conference room.

"*Have you spoken with your buddies today?*" Valeria asked.

"*Only Commissioner Hunt,*" Angela said. "*But I didn't say much because he brought up something Mr. Percy had told him that made me feel a bit uncomfortable.*"

"*Shh,*" Valeria whispered. "*He's behind us.*"

Angela and Valeria then stopped to wait for Commissioner Hunt so they could walk in together. As they were walking past the men's restroom, Jerry came out and joined them. When they entered, Commissioner Hunt proceeded to the head table and sat next to Chairman Robertson, who was looking through the pile of documents that had been placed before him. Jerry, Angela, and Valeria proceeded around the standing crowd and took seats along the sidewall where they could observe individuals coming in. Occasionally, upon noticing members of the opposing team walk in, Jerry or Valeria would nudge Angela who was seated between them. As they sat watching the smirked expression on Commissioner Hudson's face as he walked around greeting members of their team, Angela whispered to Valeria, "*I'm confident that something is up.*"

"*I agree, watch how Commissioner Hudson taps on his briefcase?*"

"*Check out Councilwoman Jones' face,*" Angela said.

"*They all seem happy. I bet they're up to something,*" Jerry whispered.

"You're right, and we'll soon find out," Angela said.

Shortly afterward, Commissioner Hudson went to the head table and spoke with Commissioner Robertson. From the expression on both Hunt and Robertson's faces, it was apparent that Commissioner Hudson said something that caused them to become uneasy. Angela then decided she needed to make many more copies of the documents. She immediately left the conference room with Valeria following her.

"Let me make the copies the meeting is about to start. You go back in."

As Angela was taking a seat Chairman Robertson started tapping on the table to get attention.

"The meeting is called to order," he said.

With all eyes on him, attendees became quiet.

"Ladies and gentlemen, I'm glad all of you could make it..; welcome."

Chairman Robertson then looked at Councilwoman Jones, who had a big smile, and said, *"That includes you, Councilwoman Jones."*

Councilwoman Jones chuckled as she acknowledged with a head bow. She was now attending the meeting as the lead person involved in the pull-out effort. Individuals in the room who were present at previous meetings she and Jason had attended before his death, chuckled. They remembered some of the allegations the two had made after leaving the meetings. One's first impression of her would leave you thinking, that she was a sweet old woman, but people who knew her were aware that she was conniving and power-driven.

Councilwoman Jones was a tall slender white female, in her mid-forties. She has long stringy auburn-colored hair. She is known for being noisy and very outspoken. She served as City Councilwoman in Douglasville, a town in Scott County

As Chairman Robertson was speaking, Councilwoman Jones watched eagerly. Those who observed her later spoke of her as being a conniving- self-centered woman.

As the meeting went forward Chairman Robertson proceeded, saying, *"I trust that all of you got your package in the mail. Are there any questions, comments, or corrections?"*

After a brief pause, he proceeded, *"If there are no comments can I get a motion?"*

A motion was given, seconded, and carried.

He then stated that Commissioner Hudson had asked to have the aging program inserted on the agenda.

Commissioner Gray then whispered to Chairman Robertson suggesting that they allow Commissioner Hudson to speak first. Chairman Robertson then asked for a motion to amend the agenda and go straight to the aging program issue. A motion was made, seconded, and the motion carried.

Commissioner Hudson proudly stood, put his left hand in his trousers pocket, and used his right hand to point as he recognized supporting team members.

"Ladies and gentlemen," he said in a confident tone, *"I want to present to the executive committee these three documents."*

He then held the papers up, waving them around to ensure everyone saw them.

"I have three resolutions, signed by the county commissioners from Cook, Scott, and Clair County."

As Commissioner Hudson began reading the resolutions, Mr. Percy sat with a stunned look. It was apparent he had not expected this would ever come about. He had told the staff and executive committee members that the effort to take the aging program had been abandoned. As everyone looked on, the camera lights focused back and forth on Mr. Percy, then quickly around the room. As pull-away team members looked on very conceitedly, it was apparent they believed they had finally succeeded in accomplishing their goal.

Considering the three resolutions had the exact wording except for the names of the counties and the county commissioners who had signed them, Commissioner Hudson chose not to read all of the wording on each but read the names of county commissioners. After he finished with the resolutions, he proceeded to read another resolution.

"This resolution states that the new organization which we will form

will be coming to the Commission to pick up everything relating to the three counties."

At that moment, Chairman Robertson interrupts by tapping on the table.

"Now, wait a minute!" He firmly stated. *"While I'm Chairman, I don't plan to allow anything to be taken from the Commission without proper documentation, and those resolutions don't give you any rights."*

While Chairman Robertson was still speaking, Angela raised her hand.

"Ms. Marshall, did you wish to say something?" The Chairman asked.

Not wanting to speak out loudly, Angela walked up to the head table and gave Chairman Robertson, Commissioner Hunt, and Commissioner Gray several pages with sections highlighted. She had written a statement across the top of the first page. *'Federal regulations prohibit them from pulling the aging program.'* Of course, that got the chairman's attention. He then asked Commissioner Hudson if he had finished with his remarks. While Commissioner Hudson was concluding, Chairman Robertson was reading the highlighted sections in the documents. After Commissioner Hudson finished, the chairman asked the attendees to excuse him for a brief moment while Angela explained something to him. As Angela was explaining the highlighted information, Valeria walked in with the copies she had made. Seeing Angela at the head table, she brought the copies up. Angela then pulled several copies out and asked Valeria to make additional copies for the crowd. While Valeria and several other staff members went to make the copies, a discussion about the pulling of the program was going on. When Valeria returned, she and the two secretaries started passing out the documents. After seeing that everyone had gotten a copy Chairman Robertson yielded to Angela to make her remarks.

Angela then proceeded to tell them that the regulations given to them governed the establishment of the Area Agency on Aging (AAA). She explained the conditions under which an AAA could be formed. She then paused to allow them to read the information she had highlighted. The sections stated that; *for a county to be designated as an AAA, it must have a population above one hundred thousand.* Angela explained that in the case of the three counties, their combined population would have to exceed two hundred thousand. She pointed out that the three counties did not have the required population. As the attendees looked at the map showing Alabama Counties, they could see the population in each county. Angela told them that there has always been an assumption that the only requirement was for the counties to sign a resolution stating they would be pulling from under the Commission. She then looked at Commissioner Hudson and addressed the issue regarding taking property. She told him that the federal regulations stated that when a program leaves or is no longer funded, equipment that costs less than $3,000 shall remain with the agency and become the agency's property. She told them that all of the furniture, equipment, etc., was the property of the Commission and was leased to the aging program. As she explained the highlighted sections in the federal regulations, murmuring started to occur. The chairman then started tapping on the table to gain attention. One of the attendees then asked for a few minutes to allow them to read the regulations and gain a greater understanding.

As the attendees read silently, Commissioner Hudson, the lawyer, Councilwoman Jones, and the other county commissioners supporting them were whispering as they read the documents. Then suddenly, Commissioner Hudson jumped up and started brushing his coat sleeve. His sleeve had made contact with the burning cigarettes in the ashtray. He had lit two cigarettes and put them in the ashtray while Angela was going over the federal regulations that disqualified them from taking the aging program.

Chapter – Twenty

EFFORTS BLOCKED

Having observed Commissioner Hudson brushing himself off, Commissioner Hunt suggested to Chairman Robertson that maybe the people needed a break. While many stayed in the conference room, others chose to go out in the corridor. Being on break, many took the opportunity to read and discuss the documents more carefully, while others stood whispering and occasionally laughing softly. Three men were standing in the corridor talking; *"I can't believe those officials failed to research the matter before presenting their case,"* one of them said.

"I bet that lawyer feels stupid," the second person said.

"I bet Commissioner Hudson feels like a fool." The third man commented.

When the fifteen-minute break was over, some returned to the conference room, while others lingered longer in the corridor chatting about the federal regulations. After everyone had finally returned, Angela was allowed to go on with her presentation. While on break, staff members passed out additional documents. Seeing that each person was looking over the material, Angela commenced speaking. She explained that the three counties had been led to believe they would get more money, but according to the formula she gave them, they would get far less.

"*Why is that?* One of the attendees asked.

Angela explained that the federal dollars were allocated based on a formula that took into account population, age, ethnicity, and poverty level. She said that it could easily be seen that Butler and Woodrow would get more money because of the number of older people in those counties. As Angela continued answering questions, the noise from the chattering began to escalate. Noticing the chattering was getting out of control again, Chairman Robertson started tapping on the desk to regain their attention. He thanked Angela for her presentation and suggested that the attendees take the regulations with them and read them so they could better understand.

One of the attendees then asked Chairman Robertson why the Commission refused to allow the three counties to pull away. Mayor Aims' proxy spoke out and said; it was his understanding that they wanted to pull away to get more money. His comment was followed by another county commissioner who spoke out and told the attendees that Ms. Marshall had proven that the three counties would get less. He said the three counties did not have the required population, which automatically prevented them from pulling away.

Immediately, Councilwoman Jones spoke out and said, "*But we can run our programs better. We're small rural counties; we know what's best for our people.*"

"*We hear you, Councilwoman Jones, but you fail to see that the counties don't have the population.*" Mr. Grey said.

Mayor Aim's proxy then asked Angela who was running the county programs. Angela informed him that the county coordinators managed the programs, and they answered to the non-profit boards they were set up under. He then asked the pull-out team members if they had planned on how they would function on less money.

Again Councilwoman Jones said, "*Oh, but we'll get more.*"

"*Councilwoman Jones, Ms. Marshall's figures, and the federal regulations show that you are mistaken.*" Chairman Robertson said.

"But we believe we're right." Councilwoman Jones stated.

"Councilwoman Jones, Ms. Marshall has federal regulations that none of you knew existed," Mayor Aim's proxy told her as he was shaking his head.

Neither of the group members commented after his statement. Commissioner Hunt then asked Chairman Robertson if he would consider a motion to table the issue for another meeting.

Chairman Robertson then called for a motion. A motion was given, seconded, and the vote carried.

Chairman Robertson then gave the group another break. After the break, the attendees started returning. The pull-out team members chose not to return after being defeated in their efforts. While standing near the elevators waiting for a member who had gone to the men's room, they talked about the regulations. One of the group members started blaming Susan, Camilla, and Lynette for their lack of knowledge. As they were talking, Angela and Valeria were returning from their break. They had earlier taken the stairway to the basement and were now returning. When they opened the door to enter the corridor, they recognized Councilwoman Jones's voice. Valeria then whispered, suggesting they be quiet so they could hear what was being said.

"Oh shit!" Commissioner Hudson commented, *"Why didn't we know some of that information?"*

"I must admit, that lady…, Ms. Marshall did her research." The attorney said.

"Yes, she was thorough." One of the county commissioners said. Councilwoman Jones then remarked, *"I can't stand Angela or Percy, and I will go to hell fighting to take that program."*

"So you weren't serious when you said we would give up if Ms. Marshall's figures were correct," the lawyer commented.

"Hell no! Never!" Councilwoman Jones said in an aggressive tone of voice.

Cheryl giggled and said; *"Didn't I tell y'all Councilwoman Jones was a fighter."*

At that moment, the individuals they were waiting for walked up and they got in the elevator.

Meanwhile, Chairman Robertson, Commissioner Hunt, Commissioner Prescott, and Jerry were headed back to the conference room. Jerry chuckled and said, *"It was good Angela had that information."*

"Where is Angela?" Commissioner Hunt asked. *"Both Percy and I need to apologize to her."*

Though the meeting was about to resume, Angela and Valeria decided not to return but went back downstairs to talk. Upon returning, they passed Lynette's office; Angela gave several quick taps on the closed door, indicating that she was entering; *"Well, ladies, I saved the program this time. Would you, by chance know their next move?"*

Camilla and Lynette looked surprised, and then Lynette giggled and said, *"You think we're behind this? What would we gain if the program left?"*

"Only time will tell," Angela said as she turned and walked away.

Several months went by without any talk of them taking the aging program. It was apparent that pull-out team members were at an impasse. Many of the team supporters had pulled away after learning it would require all five counties to pull out, and Butler and Woodrow County Commissioners had made it clear they would not pull away.

Woodrow County was the largest of the five counties. The aging program coordinator, Velma, had expressed interest in pulling away earlier. Knowing Velma as well as she did, Susan believed that if they could gain Velma's support, they would have a greater chance of taking the program. Susan then called Velma and invited her to lunch. During their get-together, Susan showed Velma a drawing of an organization chart and explained how she would benefit if Woodrow County pulled from under the Planning Commission. Susan told her that Woodrow County would get an additional $150,000 more than they were currently receiving. That figure got Velma's attention, but she could not make that decision on her own, so she promised Susan she would go to her program board and talk to them.

During the time Susan was waiting to hear from Velma, a problem in Velma's financial reporting came to light. Though the problem had existed for months, and Lynette was aware of it, she had chosen not to report it to Angela. The problem was Velma was taking money from the participants' contributions and using it to cover her expenses.

Angela, wanting to know how the changes she was implementing affected the participants, would often visit the senior centers. During one of her visits to the Jasper Center, the program bookkeeper approached her and started talking about the increase in the participants' contributions. She began praising Angela for the changes that had come about under her administration. She told Angela that she had created charts, so Velma could use the charts to brag at the county coordinators' meetings. She then excused herself and went to her office to get copies of the charts to give Angela. The charts showed the increase in contributions the participants were making. Even though Angela was unaware of the increases, she never let on; she smiled and cheered the senior participants.

Immediately after returning to the office, she pulled several months of Woodrow County's Aging Program financial reports. Upon reviewing the data, she could see that the information given to her by the program bookkeeper was different from the information in Velma's reports. She then called Lynette in to discuss the findings.

"So you're just discovering that? I've known it for months." Lynette chuckled and said.

"Why didn't you bring it to my attention?"

"It's her program money," Lynette said in a haughty tone.

"I can't believe you knew that Velma was stealing, and you refused to tell me."

"How did you find out?" Lynette asked.

"It doesn't matter."

"Well, you'll have to deal with that," Lynette said.

Being somewhat annoyed by Lynette's statement and her mannerisms, Angela told her that she was disappointed by her actions. Lynette smirked and said, "When Susan was our director, we kept her informed."

"Susan is no longer the director," Judy told her.

"I know that," Lynette said.

A brief discussion between Angela and Lynette commenced, with

Lynette reminding Angela that she was always emphasizing that the counties were independent contractors. After they had concluded their discussion, Lynette left. Judy, who was standing in the doorway, watched Lynette as she walked past Camilla's office.

"*I can't believe that,*" Judy said.

"*What?*" Angela asked.

"*Lynette gestured for Camilla to follow her.*"

"*They'll probably go downstairs to laugh about the situation,*" Angela said.

"*You're right, and I bet they'll call and tell Susan,*" Judy said.

"*No doubt they will.*"

"*How do you plan to handle the situation?*"

Angela told Judy that she would have to decide after she had prayed about the matter and determined the amount of money stolen. The two then decided to meet later that evening to review the documents. After everyone had left for the evening, Angela and Judy pulled all the reports to review and compare the information. After they had finished, they could see that Velma had taken more than twenty thousand dollars over fifteen months. Angela was very disturbed by the findings, and Judy could see it. They both concluded that Lynette had been holding on to the information in hopes that they could use it as a bargaining tool when needed.

Chapter – Twenty-one

Thursday morning, Angela called Velma to schedule a morning meeting, but Velma informed her that she would not be available. Being determined to confront Velma about the reporting problems, Angela suggested that they meet later that evening. Knowing that Angela was aware of the reporting problems, Velma told her she would be busy all day. Velma then suggested meeting the following week in Birmingham, but Angela wasn't willing to wait. Feeling pressured, Velma told Angela the meeting wasn't necessary because she had put the money back into the program's bank account. Velma's statement caught Angela by surprise.

"What money are you talking about?" Angela asked, pretending as if she didn't know.

"I'm aware you were asking questions about my income statements."

"Yes, but I ask questions about each program's financial reports."

"I told you, I put the money back into the bank account."

"That's good, but we need to talk about it."

"Well, if you insist on coming, I'll see you tomorrow."

Angela would later learn that after the bookkeeper had given her copies of the income sheets, she had told Velma. Knowing Angela would have verified the information, Velma borrowed the money and replaced what she had stolen. She had even gone a step further. She had told the program board officers a lie; stating that she had a family emergency to come up but did not have the money, so she had used the program money but later replaced it. Knowing her actions were wrong, she asked the board for their forgiveness and promised she would never do it again. Believing, the lie, the program board officers accepted her statement without question.

That Friday morning when Velma got to work, Angela was waiting in the parking lot. When they got inside, they immediately started discussing the financial reporting discrepancies. Angela told her that she planned to talk to the program board officers and make them aware of the problem. Velma didn't seem disturbed by Angela's remarks; as a matter of fact, she spoke boldly, telling Angela she was ready to go to the board chairman with her. Hearing how confident Velma was, Angela decided to take a different approach. She surprised Velma by telling her that she would first want to talk to the county commissioners to see how they wanted to handle the problem. Velma's boldness quickly faded, and she began pleading with Angela asking her not to report the matter. She went so far as to take out paperwork to show Angela that she had replaced all the money. After further discussing the matter and believing Velma was truly sorry, Angela felt the need to pray about the matter before taking it to the program board.

Before learning about the misuse of funds, Angela and Velma had maintained a good working relationship, and Angela felt she owed Velma a second chance. After talking a while longer, Angela informed Velma that she would not go to the county commissioners.

A week later, after Susan hadn't heard from Velma, she again called Velma to find out if she had met with her program board. Velma told Susan that something had come up that prevented her from discussing the matter with the board. Being eager to move forward, Susan scheduled another lunch meeting with Velma. On the day of their meeting, when Velma showed up at the restaurant, she was surprised to see that Susan was accompanied by Councilwoman Jones. Aware that the problems regarding her misuse of funds would eventually come to light, Velma decided to tell them her side of the story. After she had told them the same lie she had told her board, they commended her. During their meeting, Susan talked about how much better off they would be after taking the program from the Planning Commission and setting it up in Scott County. She again talked about the $150,000 Woodrow County would get. She encouraged Velma to speak with the program board, telling her that if Woodrow County decided to pull out Butler County would have no choice but to come along. Hearing this, Velma believed she could go to her board with that information and persuade them to make the move.

The board was made up of both Black and White members. They were all in their late sixties, seventies, and early eighties. Velma had built a good working relationship with them; she had them wrapped around her little finger. She made sure they attended all of the senior gatherings. At the gatherings, Velma praised them and made it appear as if they were in total control of the program, and without them, the services would not exist.

Velma, believing she could talk her board into joining the pull-out team, called a board meeting. On the day of the meeting, when she started talking about pulling away from the Planning Commission, board members were very surprised. They told her they would first want to speak to the county commissioners before making that move. The board chairman told her they would get back with her after talking to Commissioner Robertson. Velma was surprised, for she had thought the board member would simply say to the county commissioners they wanted to pull away. With this new understanding of the board's relationship with the county commissioners, Velma withdrew her suggestion.

Meanwhile, presuming that Velma had been successful in talking the program board into joining forces, Susan and Councilwoman Jones now thought they had another opportunity to take the program. Their only problem was going back to Cook and Clair County Commissioners and letting them know that they had gotten Woodrow County to agree to join them. Unfortunately, they were unaware that Velma had not succeeded in getting her board's approval.

With their chance of pulling out stirred up again, Camilla and Lynette started going out, creating problems with the county coordinators. They hoped that their actions would cause the coordinators to go to their boards and complain about how the Planning Commission was mistreating them.

Several weeks later, Angela received a phone call from Marcella, the Cook County Program Coordinator. Angela and Marcella considered themselves to be close friends. During the call, Marcella asked if they could meet that afternoon at their favorite restaurant. Their private talks away from others allowed Marcella to keep Angela informed on what was going on in Cook County. Later that day, during their meeting, Marcella told Angela that her board and the county commissioners were again receptive to pulling away after hearing that the group had gained support from Woodrow County. Angela was surprised, for she was unaware that Woodrow County Commissioners had changed their mind. Seeing Angela's expression, Marcella asked if she was telling her something she hadn't heard.

"Believe it or not, this is news to me."

"What do you think will happen?" Marcella asked.

"I have no idea."

Marcella then told her that the Republican County Commissioners were talking about going to the governor and asking him to take the program and put it in Scott County. She told Angela that she had spoken with two of the Cook County Commissioners, and they told her they couldn't stop the movement. Remembering that Angela had been able to block the transfer more than a year earlier, Marcella wanted to know what Angela was planning to do. When Angela told her she couldn't block what was inevitable. Marcella became very emotional; her eyes began to fill with tears.

"Our friendship is important to me. I wouldn't want you to think I was running out on you." Marcella said.

Angela reached across the table, took hold of Marcella's hand, and said, *"This is something we have no control over."*

Angela then told Marcella she would fight with federal and state regulations as long as she could, but she knew there would come a time when the regulations wouldn't matter. She told Marcella that if Woodrow County agreed to pull out, Butler County would be forced to join the group.

"I hope that won't happen," Marcella said as she dried her tears.

"Don't worry, we'll be okay, and I trust our friendship is strong enough to survive," Angela said.

"It is," Marcella said with a smile.

As they continued talking, Marcella expressed her uneasiness about working under Camilla, Lynette, Councilwoman Jones, and Cheryl. She told Angela that she had expressed her concerns to the Cook County Commissioners, and they assured her that they would try to make sure not one of the people involved in taking the program would be put in a management position.

"That's good to know," Angela said.

After talking a while longer, the two paid their tabs and left. As they walked to their cars, Marcella looked at Angela and said, *"I believe they will succeed this time."*

"Don't worry about it; we'll be okay," Angela told her. *"Remember that Serenity Prayer on my office wall."*

The two then started reciting the prayer; *'God grant me the serenity to accept the things I cannot change, courage to change the things I can, and wisdom to know the difference.'*

As weeks passed, not hearing anything, Mr. Percy was certain that the effort to take the program had been abandoned. But that was not the case; the Republican County Commissioners in three of the five counties were meeting behind closed doors to work out a plan. At some point, they decided to go to the governor for help. They believed all they needed to do was ask Governor Hanson to transfer the Aging Program to Scott County and it would be done. They had already gone through several humiliating defeats in their effort to pull away, and they believed that Governor Hansen could force Woodrow and Butler County to join the three. They didn't realize the complications involved, nor were they aware that the governor did not have the absolute power to force the two counties to join the three.

When the Republican County Commissioners went to Governor Hanson with their request, he told them he would have the state attorneys look into the matter and get back to them. After the Governor's legal advisors had done their research, they realized the task would be difficult but possible. An assessment would have to be done by a state board to determine the feasibility of moving the program. Governor Hanson then assigned the task to the State Commission on Aging Board (SCOAB). The board's mission was to look into the matter and advise the governor on what actions to take. They were to listen to the voices of the people and make a decision based on the best interest of the population being served.

The nineteen-member state board had been appointed nearly three years earlier, but no one in the aging network had ever observed the board in action, nor had board members been seen together. The Commission on Aging had gone through a financial crisis with the Medicaid Waiver Program, but it was not the state board that solved the problem; it was the work of the aging network task force.

When the names and credentials of the state board members were publicized, many people in the aging network began talking about them. The makeup of the board included; doctors, lawyers, retired educators, businessmen, state legislators, and state cabinet members. Four of the nineteen members were selected as board officers. Dr. Banks, a well-known physician at one of Birmingham's hospitals, was appointed as board chairman. He was a tall, medium-built White male in his late sixties. He was known to be a fair-minded man. Ms. Waters was a Black female in her early seventies. She was a retired high school principal. She was known to be a woman who would speak out for what she believed was right. Mr. Williams, a Black man, and Mr. Smith, a White man, were both in their mid-seventies. They were both practicing attorneys.

After Mr. Percy had read the newspaper and saw their credentials, he was sure that well-educated, intelligent people would make the right decision.

Immediately after coming together, the state board held their first meeting. Participation was limited to state board members, several COA staff members, the Planning Commission Executive Director, Ms. Marshall, the county programs board officers, the county commissioners from the five counties, pull-out team members, and a few other officials. The case was presented by Commissioner Hudson and Councilwoman Jones, who were members of the pull-out team, being opposed by Ms. Marshall, the Planning Commission AAA.

Immediately after being notified of the upcoming meeting, Ms. Marshall sent copies of all the state and federal regulations that governed the requirements for eliminating one AAA and establishing another to replace it. In addition, she sent information about their establishment, policies, and regulations. Having read the information and doing further research the state board members were somewhat knowledgeable of the problem.

After listening to both sides being presented, state board members began asking questions. From the answers received they were able to assess the problem and make their decision. Dr. Banks stated that they saw no reason to prolong their decision, and the board had agreed that no change in relocation was necessary.

After a few additional comments, the meeting adjourned.

Chapter – Twenty-two

COUNTY COORDINATOR FIRED

Having lost another battle, Susan was unwilling to concede, so she pleaded with Scott County Republican County Commissioners asking them to go back to the Governor. After some time had passed Commissioners Hudson and several other Republican County Commissioners decided to go back to the Governor. The Governor then gave the COA State Board the mission of finding a reason to give the aging program to Scott County.

Being asked to go against their initial findings and make a decision they believed was wrong, the state board held another meeting to decide how to resolve the problem. To demonstrate their fairness, the second meeting was attended by a larger group of people, which included the Executive Directors of the Council of Governments, from around the state.

When Angela walked into the conference room, she was surprised to see the large crowd. Among the crowd was a sizeable number of elderly citizens the Scott, Clair, and Woodrow County Coordinators had recruited and brought in. Their goal was to show the state board that they met the required qualifications. They had also told the seniors what to say. During the meeting discussion, several seniors got up and spoke. They informed the state board that they wanted their programs managed by country people rather than big-city people in Birmingham. They went on to say country people understand country people better. During their presentations, Angela and Valeria looked on in disbelief. The two were dumbfounded by what they were hearing. After hearing the presentations, a prolonged discussion was carried on before the Board adjourned.

As Angela and Valeria walked to the car neither said a word. Upon approaching the car, Angela threw the keys to Valeria and asked her to drive. Once they were on the highway, Valeria started tapping on the steering wheel and screaming with laughter.

"*Say it! Go ahead and say it! I know you want to say it.*"

In a loud voice, Angela began yelling, "*Where in the hell did they find all those older Black people? I've never seen any of them before today.*"

"*I knew you would say that,*" Valeria said as she laughed. "*I'm in the counties more than you are, and I have never seen that many older Black people in the senior centers.*"

"*I can't wait to get back to the office and check the census report. I didn't know we had that many Blacks in those counties.*" Angela said.

"*And certainly not in Scott County,*" Valeria added.

"*You're right; that county is almost predominantly White.*"

The two then started talking about Velma's arrogance when the seniors from Woodrow County were talking. They concluded that Velma must have recruited her, considering, so few Blacks attended the senior centers.

"*Did you notice the expression on Commissioner Robertson's face when the seniors from Woodrow County were speaking?*" Valeria asked.

"*Yes, and I can't wait to get back and talk to him.*"

Angela then reminded Valeria about the program funds Velma had stolen. She told Valeria that she had spoken with Commissioner Robertson and Commissioner Hunt and talked them into giving Velma another chance and allowing her to stay.

"*Velma is not a county employee; what can they do?*" Valeria asked.

"*They will have to get the program board to fire her.*"

"And you think the board will do it?"

"Yes.., the county commissioners appointed that board."

"I wish I could be present when they fire Velma."

"Don't worry; I'll tell you everything."

The two talked and laughed as they drove back to Birmingham.

Later that evening, shortly after 6:30 p.m., Angela received a conference call from Commissioner Robertson and Commissioner Hunt.

"What are we going to do about Velma?" Commissioner Hunt asked.

"Do you want her out?" Angela inquired.

"Sure, we don't need a coordinator who will go against our wishes." Commissioner Robertson said.

"What do we have to do to get rid of Velma? She's not a county employee." Commissioner Hunt stated.

"You're right, but the county commissioners formed the board she is employed by." Angela reminded them.

"You're right, that board was set up by our predecessors." Commissioner Hunt said.

"Angela that board will have to find a replacement for Velma." Commissioner Robertson stated.

"I'll take care of that," Angela assured them.

Angela told them that Juanita, Velma's assistant, would make a good county coordinator.

"Do you think she can handle the job?" Commissioner Hunt asked.

"She's good, and she would be a great coordinator," Angela told them.

Commissioner Hunt then told Angela they would call the other county commissioners and the program board chairman and set up a meeting.

"We want you to come to the meeting." Commissioner Robertson said.

After talking for a while, Angela agreed to meet them the following morning at 9:00 a.m... After they had concluded their discussion, Angela called Valeria.

When Valeria answered, she was laughing.

"Angela, I told my husband it was you calling. Did you talk to the county commissioners?"

"Yes, and tomorrow will be Velma's last day."

"Tell me what they said?"

With excitement in her voice, Angela proceeded to tell Valeria the details of her conversation with the county commissioners. Angela said that Commissioners Robertson and Hunt were outraged by Velma's appearance at the meeting. The fact that she had gone out and gathered all those Black seniors and bused them in had truly pissed them off.

"I was looking at Commissioner Robertson and Hunt when the black lady from Carbon Hill was speaking. You could tell they were not pleased." Valeria said.

Angela giggled and said. *"Well, you'll have to give the coordinators credit. They went out and found their poor elderly minorities."*

"Angela, I don't remember them calling on either of the White seniors to speak."

"They didn't."

"Wasn't that discrimination, busing them in but not allowing them to talk?" Valeria said with a short chuckle.

Before terminating the call, Angela told Valeria that she would tell her everything after returning from Woodrow County the following day.

The following morning Angela was at the courthouse waiting for the meeting to start. Angela could see that all of the aging program board members and county commissioners were present. After the meeting got started, the county commissioners told the board members what Velma had done and how much it had hurt them to learn that she was working behind their backs. Commissioner Robertson asked the board members who had permitted Velma to join the pull-out team. When the board members told the commissioners that they were unaware of Velma's actions, Commissioner Hunt stated, *"So you're telling us… that she went behind your back!"*

"Now, if she was a county employee, we would fire her on the spot," one of the other county commissioners said.

Commissioner Hunt and Robertson then talked about the money Velma had taken from the program. Considering she had put the money back into the account, they had felt sorry for her and allowed her a second chance. As Commissioner Hunt talked, he didn't go into details, telling them the amount of money taken and the period Velma had been taking the money, mainly because he, Angela, and Commissioner Robertson were embarrassed that they had allowed her to stay after she had cried.

One of the commissioners then said, *"We should have gotten rid of her at that time."*

After they had each expressed their feelings, the aging program board chairman immediately called for a motion to terminate Velma. The motion was made, seconded, and approved by all of the board members.

After the meeting was over, Commissioner Hunt and the aging board chairman, Mr. Hudson went to the senior center where Velma's office was located. They informed Velma that the board members were not pleased with her actions, and they had met with the county commissioners discussed the issue, and voted to terminate her. She was then told to pack her personal belongings and leave the building.

Meanwhile, as they were taking care of Velma, Angela was meeting with Juanita giving her all the details and encouraging her to take the job when offered. After the county commissioner and the aging board chairman had finished dealings with Velma, they called Juanita in and offered her the position, and she accepted.

After getting back to the office, Angela immediately went to Valeria's office. Before Valeria could say anything, Angela greeted her with a big smile and said, *"Oh well... problem solved, you must go to Woodrow County and meet the new county coordinator."*

"Girl... I want to hear all the details." Valeria said.

Angela and Valeria then went down the hill to the park. As they walked, Angela gave Valeria an account of all the details.

Several weeks later, Ms. Waters and Mr. Williams two of the state board officers came to the Planning Commission to talk with Angela. They told her they had not been able to make a decision, and they were traveling through the region, visiting the senior centers to get input. The problem they were running into was they had visited all of the senior centers in the three counties but could not locate the seniors who had spoken at the last meeting. Ms. Waters told Angela that they had talked with many seniors, but none of them knew the seniors they were looking for.

"*Do you know which centers they attend?*" Mr. Williams asked.

"*No, I can't help you. Before the meeting, I had never seen any of those seniors.*"

"*Hum,*" Mr. Williams said with a slight chuckle.

Angela went on to tell them, there were so few black seniors attending the centers she knew them all by name.

"*Well…, if you don't know them, and the people we talked to didn't know them, where did they come from?*" Mr. Williams asked.

"*Perhaps you should be asking the county coordinators.*"

"*We wanted to, but no one knew the whereabouts of the former Woodrow County Coordinator?*" Ms. Waters said.

"*Do you know how we can locate her?*" Mr. Williams asked.

"*No, I don't,*" Angela said.

"*What happens to her, I wonder.*" Mr. Williams said as he was looking at Angela over the top of his glasses.

But Angela refused to comment. Looking at each other, Mr. Williams and Ms. Waters then smiled.

As they continued talking, Mr. Williams's attention was drawn to the awards on Angela's walls. He then stood and walked over and started reading the comments. In addition to the Army Achievement, Army Commendation Medals, and State Beauty Pageant awards, Angela had numerous other awards and plaques recognizing her achievements in other areas. As he stood reading the wording, he congratulated her, telling her he understood why the pull-out team members had to go to the Governor for help.

Mr. Williams then told Angela that they had been told she was a fighting woman, and so far, they had seen her in action.

Ms. Waters commented, "*You have given the pull-out team members a helluva fight.*"

Angela smiled and said. "*Just stating facts and figures.*"

"Sure," Mr. Williams said.

He then informed Angela that they had found no reason to take the program, but given that the Republican County Commissioners were pleading with Governor Hanson, the Governor would most likely tell the board to recommend removal. He then paused and looked at Angela to see the expression on her face.

"I wouldn't want to be in your position," Angela said.

"Why is that?" Ms. Waters asked.

"When they get the program and learn there is no more money, they're not going to be satisfied."

"We know that." Ms. Waters said. *"We have spoken to Mr. Wilson at COA."*

"You're right. The money isn't in the budget, but they believe it is." Mr. Williams said.

As they continued talking, Angela was somewhat reluctant to express her true feelings, considering the Planning Commission was governed by all the county commissioners in their region. However, one of them brought up an issue that allowed her to present some information. She then took out some large envelopes which contained newspaper articles she was keeping. She had highlighted sections she believed would be valuable to her in the future. As they read some of the articles, Ms. Waters commented: *"Scott County is a mess. Those county commissioners seem to be at odds about everything."*

Mr. Williams looked at Ms. Waters and Angela and said with laughter. *"Good old southern politics."*

Mr. Williams then looked at the clock, noticing the time; he apologized for dropping in unexpectedly. After a few other comments, they left.

Chapter – Twenty-three

PROMISES TO SWAY BOARD'S DECISION

A short time later, Angela and Valeria were sitting on a park bench talking. Angela was telling her about her conversation with the two state board officers. She told Valeria that the program would be taken.

"The board members seem like intelligent people; they may not recommend removal," Valeria said.

Angela laughed, *"You've been listening to Mr. Percy too long. They told me they would more than likely recommend removal."*

Angela reminded Valeria that three counties were controlled by Republicans, and their state Governor was a Republican.

"So you think, it's that simple?"

"Yeah," Angela said with a chuckle.

By the time the state board got around to its third meeting, more than three months had passed. Having been forewarned that the board would give the program to Scott County, Angela was spiritually and emotionally equipped to accept the decision. Not only had she prepared herself spiritually, but she had also started applying for other types of funding to make up for the loss of the aging program grant.

On the day of the third meeting, Dr. Banks walked into the COA

Conference room, greeting people as he passed. The room was filled; standing near the doorway were Republican members of the Senate and House. Standing beside them were members of the pull-out team. After Dr. Banks had taken his seat and greeted the crowd, he opened the meeting for discussion. He stated that he and the board members had met and discussed whether or not to take the aging program from the Planning Commission and give it to another agency to administer. He told the attendees that he and other board members had spoken to each of the five county coordinators and had gotten different responses to the questions they asked. He stated that the county coordinators' main issue was the amount of money they were getting. Dr. Banks went on to say that board members had learned that before the appointment of Ms. Marshall, a few of the county aging program staff saw themselves as employees of the planning commission, but they weren't given the same benefits. However, after Ms. Marshall's appointment, she made it clear that they were employees of the non-profit boards in their counties, and subject to the policies and regulations established by the non-profits.

As he continued discussing the misconceptions the state board had learned about, he looked at Ms. Marshall and said, *"Ms. Marshall, we know you are a knowledgeable, respectable AAA, and the county's desire to pull away is by no means a reflection; of your leadership."*

He then went on to talk about many of the things Ms. Marshall had accomplished while working with the five counties. He talked about the trips she had taken the coordinators on and the grants she had helped them write. He said she had done many things to improve and expand services and help the programs increase participant numbers.

He then stated, *"Let it be noted in the minutes. Their desire to come from under the Planning Commission is based solely on money."*

As he proceeded to talk about the money and how it was awarded, he pointed out that the coordinators believed they would be able to get more money if they pulled from under the Planning Commission. He stated that their beliefs were based on the amount of money the AAA paid in, indirect costs, the aging staff salaries, and benefits. He then

told the attendees that the board would be making a decision that some
would like, whereas others would not.

With that statement; Commissioner Hudson then raised his hand;
Dr. Banks recognized him and allowed him to speak. Before starting his
remarks, Commissioner Hudson got several team members to pass out
handouts. When Angela got her copy and started looking at the information, she was astonished by what she was reading. As Commissioner
Hudson began to explain, he stated that after the program transfer…

He was then quickly interrupted by one of the board members who
cautioned him on the phrase *'after the program transfer,'*

After several people chuckled, Commissioner Hudson proceeded.
He stated that in the event the program was given to Scott County they
would annually save $90,000. He was assuming that the aging program
was paying the Planning Commission that amount for rent. He was
unaware that the Planning Commission was paying $90,000.00 to the
Magnolia Company that owned the building and that money was coming from the in-direct funds.

He went on to explain that, being a small rural county, the aging program staff would be paid at a lower level than the Planning
Commission pays their employees. He had highlighted the amount of
money he believed was Angela's salary. He said that the program staff
would drive their vehicles and be paid mileage at a lower rate. As he
continued providing incorrect information, Angela sat with a look of
disbelief on her face. Dr. Banks, noticing the expression on Angela's face,
interrupted Commissioner Hudson and asked Angela if she wanted to
dispute any of the information. Angela shook her head, indicating she
did not wish to speak. However several state board members strongly
encouraged her to speak up, stating that they wanted to hear all the
information, not just one side. After much encouragement from board
members, Angela proceeded to speak. She told them that all the information on the pages the team had passed out was grossly incorrect.
She went on to say that the fact that team members believed what they
were presenting to be true was mindboggling. She chuckled, looked at

Commissioner Hudson, and stated: *"When Scott County gets the program and learns the truth, your group will be devastated."*

While Angela was still speaking, several members of the pull-out team were whispering among themselves. Assuming they may have something to say, Dr. Banks asked Commissioner Hudson if he wanted to dispute anything Ms. Marshall said. Commissioner Hudson then turned and looked at Councilwoman Jones, who quickly stood up to speak. *"Ms. Marshall is partly correct about a few things but we are small rural counties, and we don't need all of the things Ms. Marshall is now paying for."*

One of the state board members then asked. *"What type of things are you speaking of?"*

"Oh, a lot of stuff." Councilwoman Jones said.

Mr. Smith, one of the board officers, asked Councilwoman Jones to explain.

"Well, you just have to know the difference between big-city and small-town living," she told them.

Mr. Smith told her he knew a little about living in big cities and small towns, but he still wanted to hear what she had to say. All eyes were on Councilwoman Jones as she attempted to tell the crowd the differences and explain how the move would be better all around. After she finished trying to explain the difference, Mr. Smith looked around at the other state board members, chuckled, and said, *"Well... I suppose we'll just have to wait and see."*

Commissioner Hudson then interrupted and told the board that Scott County would be picking up all the costs not shown in their handouts.

"Explain that!" Mr. Williams said.

Commissioner Hudson then said that Scott County would provide the program with free space and all their utility expenses for five years. Hearing that statement, most of the people in the room gasped, while others spoke out, stating that it was a good deal.

Another board member looked around at the others and stated:

"Make sure that statement is put in our minutes so we can hold Scott County accountable."

Ms. Waters then asked: *"What will happen after the five years?"*

Commissioner Hudson went on to say that after Scott County's term was up, Cook County would take the program.

"Say what!" Ms. Waters expressed. *"So you're telling the board that the aging program will leave Scott County and move to Cook County!"*

"Yes, ma'am, Cook County will get the program after Scott County term is up." Commissioner Hudson boldly said.

Another board member then asked Cook County Commissioners to confirm what had been said. One of the Cook County Commissioners stood up and said, they were hearing things they were unaware of and Cook County had not agreed to provide free space and all the other things. He concluded stating that they had been assured that the program would be self-supporting. After he had sat down, he whispered to another Cook County Commissioner, saying; *"We should leave that damn program with the Planning Commission."*

Mr. Williams looked around the room and told them he didn't believe they had weighed all the odds. He went on to say that county commissioners can be voted in and out of office, and new county commissioners may not choose to take on those financial responsibilities.

Commissioner Hunt stood and stated, *"Woodrow County does not wish to pull out, and we feel as if they were being led away captives."*

Commissioner Prescott from Butler County followed up expressing the same sentiments. Not wanting to be left out, Commissioner James from Clair County, stood and stated, *"Being one of two democratic county commissioners, my vote didn't matter. But, I will say, y'all are making a huge mistake following Councilwoman Jones."*

After all the statements had been made, one of the board members told the pull-out team that the state board would be watching them and making sure they kept their promises, if... the program got transferred.

Dr. Banks then looked around the room and asked if there were any further comments. With no further comments, the meeting was adjourned.

On their way back to Birmingham, Angela and Valeria stopped off to have lunch with Marcella and to bring her up to date on what had been said. Unlike the other county coordinators, Marcella did not attend the state board meetings. She would always say it was not in her character to sit back and watch a group of people destroy themselves. After they had talked for a while, Angela and Valeria left.

Mr. Percy had gotten back hours earlier and was waiting for Angela and Valeria to return so they could have a staff meeting. The staff had been asking questions about what had been said, but he had chosen to wait for Angela. After Angela and Valeria returned, a meeting was called. Once they were all gathered in the conference room, the discussion started. Mr. Percy started by giving the staff an upbeat summary of the details. As he spoke, Angela and Valeria looked on with an expression of disbelief. From what he said, one would have assumed they had attended a different meeting. He said things that gave the staff the impression that the program would not be taken. Seeing the expression on Angela's face, Jerry wanted to hear what Angela had to say. Angela chose not to go into details about who said what but went straight to the point and told the staff that the program would be taken. She reminded them that all of the members of the state board were Republicans, and Scott County had converted to a Republican county.

Mr. Percy interrupted and said: *"Let's not make those assumptions. The board is made up of intelligent, well-educated sensible-minded people. You could tell from the comments they were making."*

Angela then reminded Mr. Percy that Scott County had successfully gotten other programs and businesses taken out of Birmingham since the election of Governor Hanson.

"But, you can't say they will pull the aging program. My executive committee will not allow them to do that."

It was apparent to Angela that Mr. Percy did not want to hear anything contrary to his belief. Hearing him say, what his executive committee would do, Angela knew there was nothing more she could say. Blair then asked Angela when they would know what the state board was planning to do. Despite the fact she had been told by two board members, she pointed to Mr. Percy to allow him to answer. Recognizing that the staff was more interested in hearing what Angela had to say, Mr. Percy asked her to respond.

"I have nothing more to say," Angela told them.

But the staff insisted on hearing her opinion.

"It is clear to me," Angela said. *"Even though we attended the same meeting, we heard different things. It sounds like Mr. Percy is sure the state board will not recommend transfer of the program, whereas I am positive they will."*

At that moment, without further discussion, Angela left the conference room with Valeria following her. The two went downstairs, sat on a bench, and talked about Mr. Percy's attitude, some of the things Commissioner Hudson and Councilwoman Jones had said, and how the attendees had responded.

"It's obvious Mr. Percy is not willing to face the fact that the program will be taken," Valeria said.

"He'll soon find out," Angela said with a chuckle.

"Angela, I don't know if he can handle the loss of the program."

"Well… we will eventually find out," Angela said.

Chapter – Twenty-four

ANNOUNCEMENT MADE

As *time went on*, Angela kept busy putting the plans together for the upcoming statewide nutrition conference, which was six weeks away. Having the responsibility for ensuring everything went well at the conference, Angela and her staff worked long hours planning for the 800 people who were planning to attend. As an unforeseen blessing for Angela, the work involved in putting on the conference took precedence over her concerns about losing the aging program. Whenever a comment was made about the probability of losing the program, Angela would tell the person that she was no longer dwelling on the issue. She had prayed and given the matter over to God and was now believing that everything would work out according to God's plan for her life.

While waiting for the final decision, Angela would sometimes get calls from Cheryl or Clara. Knowing that the state board decision would alter their working relationship Angela never displayed any harsh feelings toward them, she continued dealing with them as she had in the past. When the transfer subject or the expected funding increase was brought up, Angela would take the time and listen. Listening to Clara talk about the money was like watching a friend step out in front of a fast-moving train and not being able to stop them.

As time passed the conference got started. The registration setup for both the training and the hotel went off flawlessly. The Wynfrey Hotel, located at the Galleria Mall had been a perfect choice. Attendees were able to shop, dine, and socialize in various locations throughout the mall, and the surrounding areas. For sightseeing purposes, Angela had arranged to have buses take the attendees on tours of wealthy communities. In addition to the other options, hospitality suites with refreshments of all kinds were set up on several floors in the hotel.

On the last day of the four-day conference, Angela was praised for the work she and her staff had done. As the afternoon training sessions were beginning, Angela observed several state board members coming in. Though their presence was not on her agenda, she believed they were there to take advantage of an opportunity to make an announcement. Later, when she spoke with Valeria, Valeria informed her that she had seen several Scott County pull-out team members talking to several state board members. Hearing that, Angela was now sure that the state board had decided to give the program to Scott County.

The remainder of the afternoon seemed to have gone by relatively slowly. Though Angela was tired and was looking forward to the closing session, she kept busy, dropping in on each session to ensure everything was going well. At some point during her rounds, she was notified that the state board was requesting time on the agenda.

That afternoon when the training sessions ended, attendees started making their way to the ballroom. It was obvious they were excited, for they were looking forward to being one of the lucky winners of the many gifts. Angela had put a great deal of time into promoting the conference to the Galleria merchants and her efforts had paid off, practically all of the businesses had donated gifts to be given away. Angela also promoted the gift giveaway session by putting pictures of the gifts in every training room.

As Angela and two of the four speakers sat on the stage waiting to get started, Angela was observing the attendees coming in. She was eager to see if Camilla and Lynette would take seats with the rest of her staff. After everyone was seated she saw that Camilla and Lynette had taken seats with members of the pull-out team. Seeing the smiles on their faces, Angela remained peaceful despite knowing the state board was there to make the announcement. As she sat looking out at the attendees she had the peace God had offered her. God's words in *Isaiah* 26:3 state that; *'God will keep you in perfect peace if you keep your mind stayed on Him.'* Angela also believed that God had used the attendees to fill her heart with joy, for she had received numerous praises regarding her planning and the execution of those plans.

After the other speaker came up and took his seat, the meeting got started. Angela then walked up to the podium to make her final remarks and thank the attendees. After her comments, the crowd gave her a standing ovation. Having the attendees show such admiration and appreciation was a God-sent blessing. After taking her seat, Mr. Percy, then the other two speakers, one after the other, got up and made their remarks. After the conclusion of the closing session, Angela informed the attendees that the gift giveaway phase was being delayed because the state aging board had asked for time to make an announcement.

Shortly after she and the others had left the stage and taken their seats among the attendees, state board members started making their way in. Not having assigned seating, board members took seats among the conference attendees. As they waited for the state board officers to make their way up to the stage, time passed. As everyone waited, looking around for Dr. Banks to make his way to the stage, murmuring started. Like the others, Angela was also looking around and wondering what was causing his delay.

At that time, Angela was unaware that state board officers were being delayed because they were attending another meeting. They were meeting with members of the Planning Commission Executive Committee and several COG Executives from around the state. They had been meeting behind closed doors for a couple of weeks negotiating on a deal that would upset many people. The delay in coming to the meeting was due to their finalizing the deal they had agreed on.

After some time had passed, Angela noticed several Republican Legislators and county commissioners from Scott, Cook, and Clair County standing near a set of doors looking out into the lobby. Then Dr. Banks and the board officers walked up. After chatting with the commissioners for a moment or two, Dr. Banks and the board officers made their way to the stage. Dr. Banks begins by apologizing for their delay. After a few other comments, he started introducing board officers and members.

As he was talking, Valeria, who was seated at the table next to Angela, whispered and told her that Commissioners Robertson, Hunt, Prescott, and several other unknown men had come in and taken seats on the back row. Angela then turned to see who the unknowns were. Seeing the smile on Commissioner Hunt's face brightened her spirit, even though she was unaware as to why they were there, seeing Commissioner Robertson gesturing to her with tight fists, provided comfort and further stabilized her positive thinking.

After Dr. Banks had finished introducing the board members, he made the announcement that many had expected. That is everyone except Mr. Percy. Dr. Banks stated that in the interest of the senior citizens in the regions, the board had voted to transfer the aging program from under the Planning Commission and give it to a newly formed organization in Scott County. At that moment, members of the pull-out team exploded with joy. They were yelling and cheering, *"We finally got it! We got it!"*

Though Angela understood their joy, she was a bit sad, but greatly satisfied to know that she had fought a good battle. As she watched them cheering she realized that their joy would soon fade.

Having interrupted his remarks with their shouts of joy, Dr. Banks stood waiting for their excitement to tone down. Moments later he started tapping on the podium to get attention. After they had quietened down, he proceeded with his remarks. He stated that the application for the de-designation process had been submitted and a transfer of the program would take place once the approval came through. He went on to say that the state board had been assured that the aging program would greatly benefit under new management, and the state board would be holding them to their promises. After he had concluded with his remarks, the meeting was adjourned.

Not wanting to keep the attendees waiting any longer, Angela quickly made her way back to the stage, pulled the curtain back, and started the gift giveaway phase. As names were drawn from the barrel and winners made their way to the stage to receive their gifts, the crowd was excited and displayed great joy.

After the session ended, a few conference attendees came up to Angela, thanked her for the job she had done, and expressed their feelings about the state board's decision. As she stood talking to different people who approached her, several state board members came up, one after the other to commend her on the successful outcome of the conference. Before walking away, a couple of them told her that everything was going to be okay, and though she didn't understand why they made that statement, she agreed with them.

After the majority of the people had left, Valeria came over to Angela and began stroking her shoulder.

"How are you holding up?" Valeria asked.

"Great!" Angela said. *"But I must admit, I'm beginning to feel like a widow at a funeral with all the people coming over and expressing their sentiments."*

The two then softly chuckled.

"That's a funny way of saying it," Valeria said. *"By the way, I saw you talking to Commissioner Robertson how does he feel about the board's decision?"*

"Everything is going to be okay," Angela said.

"Are you not upset?" Valeria asked.

"No," Angela said with a smile.

Valeria and Angela had talked frequently about the probability of losing the aging program and Valeria was aware that Angela had already started preparing for the loss. Angela had applied for, and been approved for grants with budgets that far exceeded the money the aging program brought in. Knowing that Valeria told Angela that she liked her attitude. As they continued talking Valeria mentioned that she had seen several COG Executives talking to three Planning Commission Executive Committee members.

"I saw them also," Angela said.

"I can imagine they are fearful of having the same thing happen in their region," Valeria said with a light chuckle.

"Perhaps not, they're no longer concerned about that. They've taken steps to discourage that from happening." Angela told her.

As they were talking, they noticed that nearly all of the people had left the ballroom, so they decided to go out into the mall and continue their conversation. As they were walking alone, Angela started telling Valeria about the things Commissioner Robertson had told her. He had told her that several COG Executives from around the state had met with him and several other Planning Commission Executives Committee members to offer their support. Knowing that Susan wanted to see all the AAAs taken from under the COGs, they came up with a plan designed to discourage their AAA Directors from trying to pull away. Their plan required the support of the state board, so they arranged to meet with state board officers. During their meeting, they laid out their plan and asked the state board to go along with them.

"Did he tell you anything about their plan?"

"Yes, they wanted to make sure that the right people served on the executive committee of the new agency, and they wanted to exclude pull-out team members from being employed with the new agency."

"Did the state board agree?"

"Yes, they did."

"Well…, that sounds like Camilla and Lynette will not be employed."

"You're right, that was their intent, to prevent all the people involved from being hired with the new agency."

Angela went on to tell Valeria that the reason the state board officers were late coming to the meeting was due to a meeting they had with the COG Executives. She said that after they had met with the members of the pull-out team, they followed up with a meeting with COG Executives.

Angela told Valeria that the new organization would be governed by twenty-five members, five commissioners from each county. Fifteen of the twenty-five commissioners would serve on the executive committee. Angela reminded Valeria of things the pull-out team had said about being different from the Planning Commission, and having only county commissioners serve on their board, sets them apart. She then gave Valeria a list with the names of all the county commissioners.

"Angela, this will put three counties against two?"

"Look at the names again," Angela said.

As Valeria read the names she said, *"I don't understand."*

Angela began to remind Valeria of other significant details of the new aging board and their committees' makeup. She told Valeria the battle was no longer Republicans against Democrats. It was now based on what was right and wrong. Angela told Valeria that all of Woodrow and Butler County Commissioners would vote together and that Scott, Cook, and Clair County Democratic County Commissioners would vote with Butler and Woodrow County.

With a short chuckle, Angela said; *"The pull-out team has no idea about the predicament they will find themselves in. They are celebrating now, but when they learn the truth their excitement will fade.*

"I wonder what Susan will do now," Valeria said.

"There's nothing she can do. She got what she fought for."

Angela then told Valeria that she had asked Commissioner Robertson to allow her to make several job referrals of people she believed would make good employees, and he accepted her offer.

Valeria then suggested that they encourage some pull-out team members to apply for positions, knowing they would not be hired.

"That sounds devious," Angela said, *"but I must admit, that's a good idea."*

As they were making their way back to the hotel, talking about things they could do, they saw Camilla, Lynette, Cheryl, Councilwoman Jones, and Susan walking toward them with expressions of great jubilation.

"Check out the smiles on their face," Valeria said.

"I see them, but remember we also have something to smile about."

As they came nearer, Angela and Valeria cheerfully greeted them.

"Angela, they think they have won."

"Yeah, they do. I would like to see their faces when they learn their plans backfired."

"I wonder what they will name the new agency," Valeria commented. *"The name is written on one of those pages."*

"QC-AAA, that's odd. What does QC stand for?"

Angela told her that it was short for Five County Area Agency on Aging.

Chapter – Twenty-Five

BETRAYERS FORCED OUT

The following week, two executive committee members came in to talk with Mr. Percy about the state board's decision. They wanted to know what impact the loss of the program would have on the Commission. Mr. Percy was unprepared to give them an answer, mainly because he had refused to consider the likelihood of ever losing the program. During Mr. Percy's discussion with the members, he told them about the Planning Commission's right to appeal. They then asked whether he was considering going through with the appeals process and he informed them that he first needed to discuss the matter with the executive committee. After further discussion, they told him they would vote with the majority.

Shortly after they left, Mr. Percy came to Angela's office to get more information about the appeals process. He told her his executive committee would fight to keep the program. As he talked, Angela was thinking about the plan already made with the state board. Though she had told Valeria, she had been asked not to disclose the information to Mr. Percy. The executive committee members who had agreed on a plan were aware that Mr. Percy would not be pleased, mainly because the plan deal did not include keeping the program with the Planning Commission.

After leaving Angela's office, Mr. Percy got the secretaries to call executive committee members to set up a meeting so he could find out if they wanted to appeal. The scheduled date for the meeting was the second Thursday, nearly ten days away. Mr. Percy was sure that the committee members would go forth with an appeal.

The following day, Angela came in early to handle a few matters relating to the conference. She stayed busy all morning making calls and writing thank you letters. Shortly after 2:30 p.m., Angela decided to take a late lunch break. When she signed out, she saw that Camilla and Lynette had called in sick.

On Wednesday morning, Camilla and Lynette came in and strolled around, pretending nothing had occurred. Knowing they were there for no good reason, the staff members who had attended the conference and watched them celebrate with the pull-out team ignored them. After being ignored all day, the two decided to leave early. The following day, the two came in and paraded around, pretending to be remorseful about the upcoming loss of the program. They went so far as to ask the secretaries if they had started looking for work elsewhere. One of the secretaries got up in Camilla's face and told her that she was no longer welcome at the Commission. Later that morning, after the information about the confrontation between Camilla and the secretary had gotten around, several staff members went to Angela and expressed their disapproval of the two being there. They told Angela that having Camilla and Lynette come in each day pretending to be remorseful was like rubbing salt into a wound. Being aware of Angela's limitations in reprimanding the two, they decided to take the matter into their own hands. After discussing their plans with Angela, they waited for the opportunity to put their plans into action.

The secretarial staff was aware that Camilla and Lynette would go down to the lower-level parking area to talk and laugh about what was going on. Knowing the time they would usually go down, several staff members went down to the parking level and waited. When Camilla and Lynette went down to the parking area, they were surprised upon seeing their co-workers approaching them. Their co-workers told them in unpleasant words and tone, that they were no longer welcome, and since they didn't have the decency to leave on their own, they would force them out. Having never experienced that meanness displayed by their co-workers, Camilla and Lynette were bold enough to tell them that they would not be forced out. Their boldness erupted into a nasty verbal confrontation, with their co-workers getting in their faces and coming in contact with their bodies. Seeing their co-workers were serious, Camilla and Lynette went back upstairs to get the remainder of their personal belongings. Knowing they would be leaving, they had already removed the majority of their personal belongings. After gathering their possessions, they were forced to turn in their door keys, name tags, and business cards. Their co-workers then accompanied them to the parking area, watched them get in their cars, and drive away. A short time later, the workers came by Angela's office and waved, saying: *"Problem solved."*

Shortly after 3:00 p.m., Mr. Percy came in. He could see that everyone appeared to be in good spirits. Angela had closed the doors to the offices previously occupied by Lynette and Camilla.

The following Monday morning, Mr. Percy called Angela to his office and asked how things were going with Lynette and Camilla.

"Ok, I suppose," Angela said with a calm expression on her face.

"They both told me how sorry they were with the state board decision."

"No, kidding," Angela said.

He then explained that he and Angela had different beliefs about Camilla and Lynette's involvement with the pull-out team. He told her that he was sure they were not involved.

"But don't worry, my executive committee will not allow the program to be taken," he said in a confident tone.

Knowing that he was unaware that the staff had forced Camilla and Lynette out, Angela said very little as he talked.

"You may not believe it, but Camilla and Lynette feel bad," he said. *"Have you noticed how quiet they are?"* He said in a whisper.

Angela did not comment, she simply shrugged her shoulders.

The following two days went by relatively quickly. The administrative staff stayed busy preparing for the upcoming executive committee meeting. Angela and Grace stayed busy gathering, labeling, and boxing materials she would give to the new organization. Though she had earlier given pull-out team members copies of federal regulations that explained what they were entitled to, team members were still under the impression they would be getting everything. As Angela worked, she frequently laughed quietly when she thought about what team members were expecting to obtain, in contrast to what they would be getting. She then thought, 'I can't wait to see the expression on their faces when they come to pick up the materials.'

A short time later, Grace came in with a stack of documents she had made copies of.

"You seem happy," Grace smiled and said.

"I'm glad it shows."

"I get the impression Mr. Percy doesn't know Camilla and Lynette are no longer with us."

"He thinks they're just being quiet," Angela said.

The next day came and went without Mr. Percy noticing anything different. He was too busy preparing for the meeting to think about anything else.

Thursday morning, the day of the meeting. Mr. Percy started making calls to ensure key members would be present. The staff had already filled the conference room with extra chairs to accommodate the expected crowd. Thirty minutes before the meeting started, Commission members began coming in. A short time later, newspapers, TV, and radio reporters arrived. When the hour arose for the meeting to get started, Chairman Robertson called for a delay to wait for the arrival of Mayor Aims or his proxy. As time passed, two Birmingham City Council members walked the halls and stayed on the telephones calling around town, trying to locate the mayor or his proxy. Mayor Aims had given Mr. Percy his word that he would vote to appeal. After an hour had gone by the meeting was called off after seeing that neither the mayor nor his proxy could be located.

Angela, Valeria, and two other aging staff members, Shelley and Belinda, left the conference room and went to Angela's office. After closing the door, they started talking about what they had just witnessed. Being a very talkative person known for expressing her feelings, Shelley did not hold back. The first thing she said was: *"It's obvious someone cut a deal with the mayor."*

"And who do you think it was?" Belinda asked.

"I don't know, but someone will benefit from the mayor's absence," Shelley said.

Shelley then told them she had overheard several people talking in the corridor. One of the city council members was telling the others that he couldn't remember a time when the mayor or his proxy didn't attend a committee meeting.

"Angela, what do you think?" Belinda asked.

"I don't know, but I have some thoughts about it."

"Well, tell us," Shelley said, *"Do you think the mayor cut a deal with Scott County Commissioners?"*

"I don't know," Angela said. *"But, I find it hard to believe; no one knew the whereabouts of the mayor or his proxy."*

"Someone knew," Valeria said with a chuckle.

Belinda then threw in her thoughts, asking what the mayor would gain by failing to vote for the appeal. Valeria pointed out that the mayor and Scott County Commissioners were always fighting about something. She reminded them about the annexations that were taking place and the other issues that were appearing in the newspapers. Shelley then commented that maybe the mayor was tired of fighting with Scott County officials and decided to let them win for a change.

As they continued discussing what may have happened, Belinda asked Angela if she thought Scott County would go after the Medicaid Waiver Program.

"All things are possible," Angela told her.

"Would you be able to fight them off if they did?" Shelley asked.

"No, the governor is paying off his political debts with favors."

At that moment Grace came in and told them to speak quietly

because Mr. Percy and several county commissioners had gone into his office which was next to Angela's.

"I wonder how Mr. Percy is going to take this, he was sure the mayor would come through for him," Valeria said.

To change the subject, Angela started telling them about a situation she was involved in that reminded her of what they had just witnessed. Angela served on a number of boards; one was the mining museum. She told them that the mayor of the city where the museum was located wanted to purchase a piece of property owned by the museum. Knowing what the mayor wanted to do with the property, several board members were against the sale. After they had told the other board members why they disapproved of selling the property to the mayor, the board members discussed the issue and decided to take a secret vote. When the votes were counted, it was apparent none of the members wanted to sell the property to the mayor. During the discussion, it had been brought out that the residents who lived in the area didn't want to see a business brought into their community, and they had spoken out against it at every city council meeting. One of the mayor's friends who served on the museum board told them that the mayor was trying to buy the property at a low cost so that he could sell it for a significant profit. Angela went on to say it was indeed an uncomfortable position for her, but she had chosen to vote with the majority.

"Why were you so uncomfortable with your decision?" Belinda asked.

"I was having to make a decision, even though I didn't have a dog in the fight."

They all started laughing.

"Angela, you love to use that slogan," Belinda said.

Angela went on to tell them that the mayor would sometimes show up at their board meetings and try to get them to have a hand vote, but fortunate, they never had a quorum when he showed up.

"Did y'all know the mayor was planning to show up at the meeting?" Shelley asked.

"Yes, we did."

Angela went on to tell them that someone in the mayor's office would always call and tip them off.

"*That proves you can't trust everybody,*" Valeria said.

"*I agree,*" Belinda commented.

"*Well, how did y'all ever get anything accomplished?*" Valeria asked.

Angela told them they would sometimes conduct business via conference calls.

Angela was then asked how many boards she served on and how she ended up serving on the boards. Angela thought for a minute then told them that she served on eight different boards. She chuckled, then told them that she believed she had been asked to serve on three of the boards because of her gender and race. She went on to say that she was the only black and only female on the three boards.

Angela concluded, telling them that after many failed attempts, the mayor finally gave up on trying to get them to sell the property.

Hearing voices in the corridor, Grace looked out the door and saw the commissioners leaving Mr. Percy's office. Shortly afterward, those who had gathered in Angela's office ended their conversation and left.

A short time later, Mr. Percy came into Angela's office, sat down raised his hands, and said, "*I would never have believed they would let me down.*"

As he talked, Angela sat behind her desk, hands folded with two fingers touching her chin and her elbows resting on the desk. As she looked at him, she could sense the disappointment and humiliation he was going through.

After making a few comments, he got up to leave, then turned and whispered: "*Do Camilla and Lynette know?*"

"*I don't know; they're not here,*" Angela said.

"*Well, they'll soon find out,*" he said as he was leaving.

Chapter – Twenty-six

SET UP TO FAIL

K nowing that the Planning Commission was required to give the new agency certain records. Angela and Grace stayed busy gathering, labeling, and packing the materials they would give to the new agency. The pickup date was scheduled for the second week in February, less than two months away.

Also during that period, the newly formed organization personnel committee was running help-wanted ads. When the ads appeared in the newspapers, pull-out team members thought nothing of it. They looked at the help wanted ads as mere procedures, considering they had already selected the people, they wanted to fill the positions. To keep everyone from knowing who was applying for the positions, the agency personnel committee had the resumes' sent to a Birmingham post office box.

When Angela saw the help-wanted ads in the newspapers, her desire to retaliate was stirred. She took the newspapers down the hall to Valeria's office, and they sat discussing how they would implement the plan they had earlier discussed. They wanted Cheryl and Clara to apply for the AAA Director's position, knowing they would go for it if they heard that the other county coordinators were applying. In light of everything that had gone on, Angela and Valeria decided it would be best if Valeria approached the two county coordinators.

Later that afternoon, Angela and Valeria sat in the conference room discussing how they would implement their plan of getting Clara and Cheryl to apply for the top job. Their plan also included getting everyone else they knew who might be eligible to apply. After they had talked and finalized their plans, Valeria decided to leave early so she could go and start working on Clara.

That evening, after Angela had gotten home, Valeria called to let her know that she had been successful. She was excited, giving Angela all the details of what had happened. She told Angela that she was surprised by Clara's lack of self-confidence. She stated that Clara didn't see herself as being qualified for the top job. She then went on to tell Angela that she had taken on the task of persuading Clara into believing that she was probably, the most qualified of the five-county coordinators. Valeria then took the time to go into a few details. She bragged about herself, telling Angela how great she was. As Angela listened to Valeria telling her what she had done, Angela expressed great excitement. Valeria said that after she had gotten Clara to talk about some of her accomplishments, Clara seemed to have enjoyed giving her more information.

"I was determined to get Clara's resume in," Valeria said, "So I started typing as Clara talked."

"So you prepared her resume?" Angela asked.

"Yes, I even took it to the post office and mailed it."

"No... You didn't."

"I did, because, I wasn't willing to take a chance on Clara changing her mind. I now believe I can sell a used car and convince the driver it's in good condition, knowing it would stop running at the next traffic light."

After they had laughed and joked around, Angela told Valeria about several people she had spoken to and encouraged them to submit their applications.

Several days later, Valeria went to Scott County to start working on Cheryl. She told Cheryl that she was aware of several people who were applying for the AAA position. Valeria then asked Cheryl if she had submitted her resume. Cheryl told her that in light of the fact, that it was presumed that Camilla would get the appointment, she had never thought of applying for the job. Valeria then started flattering Cheryl for being selected as interim AAA Director and told her that she doubted that any of the people who were applying were as qualified as she was. As Cheryl and Valeria talked, Valeria told Cheryl that she wouldn't be surprised to hear that the other county coordinators had applied.

"You think they would apply?" Cheryl asked Valeria.

"Why not?" Valeria said. *"In light of the fact you are performing the job, I think you should submit your resume,"*

Several days later, Cheryl called Angela and told her that she was thinking about submitting her resume for the AAA position after being encouraged by Valeria. As Angela listened, Cheryl talked about her uneasiness in light of the fact Camilla was expecting to be appointed. Knowing Angela had been in a similar situation when she applied for the AAA position, she asked for Angela's opinion. Angela suggested that Cheryl pray over the matter, then maybe she would be more at ease about her decision. As they talked, Angela decided to give Cheryl some encouragement. She told Cheryl she would make a great director. She complimented Cheryl on being chosen to serve as interim AAA. After talking for a while, Angela began to feel a bit remorseful, knowing she and Valeria were setting Cheryl and Clara up for a big disappointment.

The following day, Angela and Valeria sat in the conference room, drinking coffee and laughing about the actions they were carrying out.

"What's next on our list?" Valeria asked.

Angela told her about several other people she had spoken to and encouraged them to submit their applications. She also told Valeria that Marcella wanted to take part in their scheme. Marcella knew many professional people who would be qualified to handle the job, so they decided she would be the right person for that area. With the two main adversaries taken care of, their goal was to make sure a lot of other qualified people applied. With Marcella working with them, she would contact people she knew and encourage them to send in their applications. After several days, Marcella called and gave Angela the names and backgrounds of the individuals she had spoken with. One of the people was Ms. Fuller. Marcella believed that Ms. Fuller was the right choice for the top position because she was a woman who wouldn't take any crap from anyone. The problem was Ms. Fuller, had no desire to leave her current position. Being curious, Angela decided to call people she knew in the county to see if they knew Ms. Fuller. When she started inquiring, she was able to obtain the information she was looking for. Everyone she talked with told her that Ms. Fuller could be hard to get along with, and she wasn't easily pushed around. This was good news; Angela was hoping they could get Ms. Fuller to apply for the top position. Trying to come up with ideas that would enable them to persuade Ms. Fuller to apply, Angela, Valeria, and Marcella spent a lot of time on the telephone. Marcella then decided she would talk with associates of hers and Ms. Fuller and get them to encourage Ms. Fuller to submit her application. A week later, after several people had spoken with Ms. Fuller, she decided to apply for the AAA Director's job. Hearing the good news, Angela, Marcella, and Valeria were elated.

When Angela and Valeria were not in the field, they would work together on strategies they could implement to enhance Ms. Fuller's chances of getting the top job. Knowing that Ms. Fuller was well known by the county officials, Marcella decided to talk to the county commissioners and encourage them to consider Ms. Fuller for the top position. During Marcella's conversations with the county commissioners, she would talk about her uneasiness with working with the pull-out team members.

The makeup of the Quinary County Aging Board was not much different from the Planning Commission Board, except for the number of members. Their board had twenty-five members, consisting of five county commissioners from each county. Their executive committee consisted of fifteen members, three from each county. Though the makeup was both Democrats and Republicans, several of the Republican county commissioners had decided to vote with their Democratic counterparts.

Not being aware of the many obstacles being laid, members of the pull-out team were very confident that things would work out to their advantage. Like Mr. Percy, they never thought of anything contrary to their plans.

Several Quinary County- Aging Board Personnel Committee members had promised Angela and Marcella that none of the people involved in taking the program would be employed by the new agency, nor would they benefit from their deeds. Those promises put the voting at eleven to four. This information gave Angela, Valeria, and Marcella several personnel committee members they could talk to. They had devised an appropriate interjection they would use when talking to QC Personnel Committee members. They would say very positive things about Ms. Fuller, emphasizing her credentials and how well she managed things. In contrast, they would downplay the qualifications of Camilla, Lynette, Cheryl, Clara, and Councilwoman Jones. They were fortunate; they didn't have to show malice toward them; all they had to do was make sure that the negative things those individuals had said or done were still on the committee members' minds.

As time passed, the de-designation process of the Planning Commission as the regional AAA was accomplished, and the newly formed organization, Quinary County was designated, the Area Agency on Aging (AAA). Cheryl, the Scott County Aging Program Coordinator, continued serving as interim AAA while the personnel committee searched for a staff. While in the position and being told that she was doing a great job Cheryl developed confidence in her abilities and decided to submit her resume. Camilla, on the other hand, also believed she would be the new AAA Director. She was going around in high spirits, telling people the job was hers. Neither Camilla nor Cheryl was aware of the many barriers being put up to block their chances of achieving their goal. Nor were they aware that the new board had already decided to bring in all new people.

The QC-Aging Program Personnel Committee met three times each week to review the massive number of resumes. To ensure things were done more privately, they arranged for their meetings to be held at different locations. When members of the personnel committee saw Ms. Fuller's resume, they responded favorably because of the many positive comments that had been made about her. After reviewing all the resumes and deciding on those they would interview. Commissioner Robertson called Angela to find out what she knew about the applicants.

Early the following morning, Commissioner Robertson called Angela then faxed copies of all the applicants, they had decided to interview. After reviewing all the information, Angela called Commissioner Robertson and made her recommendations. Two weeks later after the committee had performed the interviews they selected the individuals they would hire to be the staff for QC-AAA. To ensure nothing would go wrong, the personnel committee called each person and informed them that they had been selected. They immediately followed up with registered letters giving the individuals more details.

Weeks earlier after being given the program, team members had decided on the individuals who would serve as a transition team. The team was to get everything in order before the chosen staff was scheduled to report to work. On the team were Councilwoman Jones, and Cheryl, they were to hire a crew who would go to the Planning Commission and get all of the aging program furniture, supplies, equipment, and files, and set up the aging offices before the hiring of the aging staff.

On the day the transition team was to pick up the program material, Angela got to work early that morning to ensure everything was in order. Shortly after 10:00 a.m., the pick-up crew arrived. After they had exchanged friendly greetings, Angela commenced to escort them down the hall to show them the boxes they would be picking up. She and Grace had labeled and boxed all the file folders they could have. They had also boxed up all the materials they were planning to put in storage. Along the walls were many boxes, giving the impression that there was a lot to be carried away. All of the boxes had color labels indicating what was enclosed. Seeing that there were six individuals on the pick-up team, Angela assumed that the four men would handle the loading. As they walked down the hall, passing Camilla's and Lynette's former offices, Councilwoman Jones and Cheryl went in to look around. They then called Cheryl, Mr. Roberts, and the three hired helpers to discuss which office they wanted to start in. While they were chatting, Angela walked away to take a telephone call. When Angela returned, Mr. Roberts asked if it would be okay for them to move the moving van to a particular location to make it more convenient for loading.

"Where are you now parked?" Angela asked.

After he had told her, Angela went to the window to look out.

Upon returning, she said, *"Gosh! That's a big truck."*

"You think so?" Mr. Robert asked.

"I told them the truck was larger enough," Cheryl said.

"So you think it will hold all of this furniture?" Councilwoman Jones asked Mr. Roberts.

Angela immediately realized they were still under the impression they would be getting everything. She then raised her hands to get their attention.

"No! No! No!" Angela said. *"The furniture stays. Only the boxes with the blue labels are yours."*

At that moment, they all seemed confused as they looked around. Seeing the expressions on their faces Angela said; *"I sent certified letters stating which materials you would be picking up."*

Councilwoman Jones then took a nasty attitude, saying, *"But we were told that everything in these offices belongs to the aging program."*

"Yes, the Planning Commission Aging Program," Angela said.

"What are you saying?" Mr. Roberts asked.

"It's no longer the Commission's program; it's QC-AAA program," Angela told him.

At that moment, Angela took great pleasure in knowing she could disappoint Councilwoman Jones. She then remembered the statement Councilwoman Jones had made months earlier: 'I can't stand Angela.'

This was the moment Angela wanted to say, 'Well, how do you like me now?'

Chapter – Twenty-seven

PROMISES KEPT

The Planning Commission had a practice of purchasing equipment with general funds and leasing the equipment to the programs to protect itself from losses when a program left. Copies of the policy had been provided to the pull-out team members on several occasions. Angela had also sent copies of those policies in a certified letter when she was notified of the pickup date.

Councilwoman Jones asked: *"Do we get any of this stuff?"*

"No!" Angela said, *"Only the boxes with blue labels."*

"Well, what about computers and typewriters?" She asked.

Again, Angela said no.

Question after question, Angela answered no, and recited the same federal regulations. After hearing her say no repeatedly, Mr. Roberts giggled as he was shaking his head, indicating that he had gotten the message.

"Ms. Marshall, tell us what we can take so we can start loading the truck." Mr. Roberts said.

"Okay!" Angela cheerfully said as she started walking around, pointing to stacks of boxes with blue labels."

"Is this all?" Mr. Roberts asked, then held his hands up and started chuckling.

"Never mind, Ms. Marshall, you don't have to repeat it."

At that moment, the guys and Cheryl started laughing.

"Well, I wish we had known this; we could have saved the money we paid to rent that big truck." Mr. Roberts said.

He then turned to Councilwoman Jones and Cheryl and asked: *"Did either of you know this?"*

While they talked, Angela went to her office to get copies of the certified letters she had sent them. The letter listed everything they were to pick up and gave names of federal regulations explaining why the Commission was to retain the furniture and things they were expecting to take away. After they read the letters, Mr. Roberts said, *"She explained everything in these letters."*

He then apologized for their misunderstanding.

"No problem," Angela commented.

After they had collected all of the boxes and left, Valeria came walking down the hall, giggling.

"Well," she said. *"I heard some of the things they were saying. I can't believe no one read the information you sent."*

"Girl..., you should see the big truck they came in," Angela said as she and Valeria hurried to the window to look out. As they watched the driver maneuvering his way out of the parking lot they both started laughing.

"Wow," Valeria said. *"They believed they would get all the aging program equipment and furniture."*

Two days later the new staff was on board. That afternoon, after the orientation of the new staff, Commissioner Hunt, Robertson, and Prescott stopped by the Commission to provide Angela with the information. When they entered Angela's office, she was standing at the window looking down at a group of small children playing in the park.

"What's up, sergeant?" Commissioner Robertson asked.

When Angela turned, she was somewhat surprised to see the three county commissioners. After closing the door, they momentarily looked at her without saying anything.

"*Well,*" Commissioner Robertson said as he exhaled. "*We tried hard, but the odds were against us.*"

Commissioner Robertson then turned and winked at Commissioner Hunt and Prescott, who was standing slightly to his rear. The two had smiles on their faces.

Commissioner Prescott said, "*Angela, not one of the people who fought to take the program, was chosen to work with the new organization.*"

At that moment, hearing those words, Angela's eyes became wet. She then took a deep breath and put her hands over her mouth. Commissioner Robertson looked at her and said: "*Now, now, Marines, don't cry.*"

Angela then smiled.

Commissioner Robertson then took out a sheet of paper with all the new employees' names and gave it to Angela. While looking at the names, she pulled several tissues from the tissue box to dry her tears.

"*This is QC- staff; there will be no changes for the next five years.*" Commissioner Hunt said.

"*Well… that is, provided they all work out.*" Commissioner Prescott added.

"*Though I'm happy, it will not be easy for them,*" Angela said.

"*We know,*" Commissioner Hunt stated.

They then told Angela that several state board officers had worked with them throughout the process and had approved their selections.

"*That new staff will be okay. We will make sure of that,*" Commissioner Prescott said.

Commissioner Hunt then said: "*Now, how does that make you feel?*"

"*Great,*" Angela said with a smile.

"*You knew we wouldn't let you down,*" Commissioner Robertson said.

As they talked, expressing admiration for her work and the battles she had gone through, Angela stood tall as if they were pinning a commendation medal to her chest.

Commissioner Hunt then said: "*You were a good director. We know what you did and all the shit you had to put up with.*"

"Four years ago, when I called you long distance and asked you to submit your application for the job, we knew we were handing you a task." Commissioner Robertson said.

"A hard task and you held on and fought a good fight," Commissioner Prescott stated.

"A hell of a fight it was," Commissioner Hunt said.

"Well, Angela, we had better get on the road; traffic is terrible this time of the evening," Commissioner Robertson said.

As they were walking toward the lobby door, Angela quickly proceeded ahead opened the door, and saluted them.

"Okay, we're out of here," they told her.

Shortly afterward, Angela went into the restroom, and sat on the sofa, with her eyes wet with tears she began praying. After she had finished praying, she went to tell Valeria the news. As they were headed down the hill to the park, Angela was telling Valeria the names of Quinary County Aging Program employees.

"We must call Marcella and let her know," Valeria said.

"I'll call her when I get home."

Angela then reminded Valeria that they had to keep the information to themselves until it was publicized in the newspaper. The following morning, Valeria came in carrying a copy of the Clair County Times. She immediately proceeded to Angela's office to show her the article.

"I stopped at a service station and got the newspaper, and after getting back in my car, I sat reading. Angela.., I cried tears of joy."

As Valeria was talking, Grace came in and gave Angela a copy of the Birmingham News.

"I can imagine how the pull-out team members feel, especially Councilwoman Jones and Commissioner Hudson," Grace said.

"Let's not forget about Lynette and Camilla," Angela said. *"We know they were wrong, but I still feel sorry for them."*

"This is not going to be a good day for a lot of people we know," Valeria commented.

"No, it's not," Grace said.

As they were talking, Jerry and Belinda walked up carrying copies of the newspaper. Belinda said, *"I would love to be a fly on the wall at Councilwoman Jones's home."*

"I can imagine Susan is truly pissed off," Jerry said. *"This is not going to be a good day for her."*

"You're right. They all thought the cards were stacked in their favor," Belinda commented.

"Yes, they did, and the sad part about it is the worst is yet to come," Angela said with a giggle.

As they were talking Angela's memories took her to the words written in Isaiah 5:16, *'They shall be ashamed and also disgraced, all of them; they shall go in confusion together...*

With all the talk going on about the write-up in the newspapers, and the telephone call coming in, Angela was unable to get any work done. She was frequently interrupted by staff members and associates around the state who were calling to talk about Camilla, Lynette, and Susan. They were saying that the three had made a fool of themselves.

Chapter – Twenty-eight

FINANCIAL PROBLEMS

Later that morning, one of Angela's friends called and invited her to lunch. Angela was delighted; she thought she would get a break from talking about the aging program and her two former employees. Two hours later, when she entered the restaurant and took a seat, her friend Vanessa immediately started talking about the articles in the newspapers. She then asked Angela how she felt about what had happened.

"Happy, that part is over," Angela said, *"but the worst is yet to come."*

"What are you saying?" Vanessa asked.

But before Angela could comment, Vanessa's attention was captured by a news reporter on the television who was talking about the QC-AAA staff.

"Several people in our office were talking about that situation this morning," Vanessa said. They all agreed that the people who fought to take the program had gotten what they deserved. She went on to say that everyone she had spoken with had said; that was poetic justice at its best.

"I hadn't thought of it that way," Angela said.

Vanessa went on to say those women were so angry they were willing to see the Commission destroyed.

"Yeah, that's what Camilla told the Commission Executive Committee."

"Yes, but look how it turned out."

As they were talking their friend Deborah came in, took a seat, and started talking about newspaper articles. Considering she was late, Vanessa began joking with her, telling Deborah that the least she could have done was say hello.

"Hello, girls!" Deborah said. *"Are y'all now satisfied?"* she added.

The waiter then came over and took their order. After the waiter walked away, they continued their conversation.

"Angela, you've been fighting with those people for a long time; I know you're happy it's now over," Deborah said.

Angela chuckled and said: *"It's not over yet, and the worst is yet to come."*

"Oh yeah, what did you mean when you said that earlier?" Vanessa asked.

"Vanessa, what are you talking about?" Deborah asked.

Vanessa then told Deborah she was so eager to tell Angela about a conversation she had with several co-workers that she failed to follow up on Angela's statement, about something she had said.

"Tell me what Vanessa is talking about?" Deborah asked Angela.

Angela thought for a moment…, then attempted to change the subject by talking about the weather. Her friends started laughing quietly.

"You are not going to change the subject that easily," Vanessa said.

For a moment, both of her friends were persistent in trying to get her to explain herself. Wanting to know what she was referring to, they started questioning her as if she was a witness.

"I'm here because I wanted to avoid talking about the aging program."

"You shouldn't have opened the door with that statement," Vanessa said.

"Let's talk about something else," Angela said.

With silly looks on their faces, they stared at her. Deborah then asked, *"What do we talk about?"*

"Okay, I get the point," Angela said.

Angela knew her friends would not let her get away with starting on a subject and then dropping it. Vanessa was an attorney, and their friend

Deborah was a counselor. Listening to them questioning her, Angela knew she had opened the door for further questioning when she made the statement. Knowing her friends were not going to end their questioning, Angela decided to explain. She told them that she was talking about the money the group was expecting.

Angela was then momentarily interrupted when the waiter approached and started placing their meals on the table. After the waiter walked away, Angela proceeded to tell them that the new agency and county programs would get less money than they were expecting. She then reminded them of some of the details she had earlier told them about the counties' statistical makeup and a few other things. Vanessa then inquired as to whether Angela would be getting a cut in salary as a result of losing the program. With a smile, Angela cheerfully told them…, no. She then reminded them of some of their earlier conversations. She told them about the various grant proposals she had submitted, that had been approved. She told them that her new grants were bringing in more money, and she was performing less work.

"*Well, that was very smart of you,*" Vanessa said.

"*That was,*" Deborah commented.

"*I was becoming concerned,*" Vanessa said, with a smile.

"*Concerned about what?*" Angela asked.

"*Whether you would have enough money to pay your bills,*" Vanessa giggled and said.

Angela chuckled and said, "*I was never worried, knowing I have good friends I could call on.*"

They looked at each other and chuckled.

"*Sure.., you could have gotten help from us,*" Deborah said as she winked at Vanessa.

Angela went on to tell them that she was blessed. She had never gone without having some type of income coming in. She reminded them of her catering business, telling them that whenever she got into financial trouble, God would always send paying customers her way.

"*All customers are paying customers, aren't they?*" Deborah asked.

"*Yes, but some brides want a champagne reception on a beer budget.*"

"Most of them do," Vanessa said.

Vanessa then started telling them about a lawsuit the mother of a bride had filed against a business. The mother had said that the business had not provided her daughter with the type of reception they had expected. She told them that the lady wanted the best of everything, but her budget was only $5,000. She went on to tell them the details of what the bride and the bride's mother wanted for $5,000.

"All of that?" Deborah said.

"Yes, all of that."

After Vanessa finished Angela started telling them about several clients she had turned down. Hearing the details Deborah and Vanessa started laughing.

After they had finished eating the waitress came over to remove the dishes and leave the bill. Deborah then quickly picked up the tickets.

"I'll pay," she told them as she took out a new hundred-dollar bill.

"Go ahead, big spender," Vanessa commented.

"You paid the last time, don't tell me you don't remember," Deborah said.

"Angela…, don't forget you'll have to pay the next time, and let me warn you now; we are going to Red Lobster at night."

After leaving the restaurant, they stood in the parking lot, talking for a few minutes.

"Thanks for the interrogation luncheon," Angela yelled as they were getting in their cars.

As time passed, it seemed as if the reporters had nothing else to write about other than the Commission losing the aging program. Not only were they, writing about the program, but the average John Doe or Mary Jane was also voicing their opinions in the editorial columns. When the reporters spoke with the agency executive committee members and asked why they had chosen people who were not involved in the pull-out effort, committee members told them, they were trying to prevent another battle from occurring. They also told the reporters that they had done a lot of soul-searching and decided to start the new organization, with all new people. They then praised the work Cheryl had done and told the reporters Cheryl was still helping the new staff. Wanting to know how Scott County residents felt about the decisions, the reporters talked to several county residents. They found that the residents agreed with the actions taken by the QC-Aging Program Personnel Committee and the state board.

The state board had also lived up to their promise ensuring the new agency got all its needs taken care of. It had been written up in the minutes, and the pull-out team had openly publicized that they would take care of everything.

To get the county residents' backing, Scott County Republican County Commissioners had made big promises, telling the citizens they would greatly benefit. They had promised county residents that the program would bring jobs to the county, but the AAA Director and her entire staff came out of Cook and Bibb County.

Earlier, when members of the pull-out team were interviewed, they had bragged about all the furniture, supplies, and equipment they would be getting from the Planning Commission. However, during the transition, they learned they would have to purchase everything for QC-AAA. This had come as a major disappointment. Even though the pull-out team was being confronted with significant losses, they were still bragging about the great program they had brought to Scott County. They were also boasting about the large budget the aging program would have.

With the QC-Aging staff in place, Susan realized her plans had not gone as expected, and Scott County Commission was having to put up a great deal of money to buy everything the new agency needed. Even worse, Susan learned that the QC-Aging Program board was made up of county commissioners she could not influence. This bad news was so devastating it sent her into a rage. Although she did not have a lot of people on the board she could put pressure on; she started putting pressure on the few she had worked with. She would visit the county commissioners in the three counties and try to intimidate them. She told them she would ensure that the agency's advance funding request was held up until she had gotten what she had fought for. To demonstrate her power, Susan stormed into the COA finance department, pulled the agency funding request forms, and started making calls. Even with her door closed, many of the COA staff could hear her yelling and making threats. Susan was telling the people she was talking to that she had taken risks for them and she expected jobs for people who had helped her. She told Councilwoman Jones and Commissioner Hudson, they had not lived up to their promises and were now on her shit list.

Knowing the scandal it would cause if the QC- AAA could not meet its payroll, nor provide funds to the county aging programs, the Republican County Commissioners got financial assistance from a wealthy Scott County citizen. With the financial issues temporarily taken care of, the Republican County Commissioners were still being pressured to hire Camilla and Lynette. Unfortunately, all of the aging program positions had already been filled.

Considering the board had more Republicans, Susan couldn't comprehend why they had gone against her wishes and hired people who were not involved in the struggle to take the program. Even after reading the article written as to why the personnel committee had hired all new people Susan refused to accept their rationale. Her unwillingness caused her to fight even more to get Camilla and Lynette hired.

On the other hand, Cook County Republican Commissioners had made a promise to Marcella, and they were holding firm to their commitment. Cook County had greatly benefitted, the majority of QC-Aging Program employees were tax-paying Cook County residents.

Early one morning, after several weeks had passed, Angela received a phone call from Marcella. Angela could sense from the sound of Marcella's voice that something was wrong. Even though they were friends, calling Angela at home early in the morning was something Marcella had never done. After hearing what Marcella wanted to tell her, they agreed to meet for lunch.

Hours later, the two were sitting in their favorite restaurant eating and talking. Marcella told Angela that Ms. Fuller was being pressured to create jobs for Camilla and Lynette. Marcella believed that, if Lynette and Camilla were hired in management positions, they would take out their frustration on her. She went on to tell Angela that her husband had suggested that she resign.

"What do you think I should do?"

"Now..., you know I'm not going to tell you what to do."

Marcella began smiling; *"Felix will be glad to hear you say that."*

As they talked, Angela reminded Marcella of one of their earlier conversations regarding other people Camilla and Lynette didn't get along with.

"I wonder how Clara will feel when she hears Ms. Fuller is being pressured to create jobs for Lynette and Camilla," Marcella commented.

"She will not like that," Angela said.

Marcella then asked Angela if she had any suggestions as to how Ms. Fuller should handle the situation. Angela told Marcella that she should talk with Ms. Fuller and give Ms. Fuller all the details. She told Marcella to tell Ms. Fuller to take caution to protect herself, not only from Camilla and Lynette but also from other pull-out team members.

Marcella then inquired as to what Ms. Fuller could do.

Angela said that, if Ms. Fuller is forced to hire them, she should start by imposing strict policies.

"What type of policies?" Marcella curiously inquired.

Angela began quietly laughing, then started telling Marcella about some of the things Ms. Henderson had done to staff members who caused problems for her. She suggested that Ms. Fuller keep them separated as much as possible and place them in a location close to her office where she could see everything they did. She went on to recommend that Ms. Fuller should have them share a telephone with another staff member and give them a lot of unnecessary work to keep them busy. Marcella started laughing as she listened to Angela, giving her a list of crazy duties Ms. Fuller could assign to Camilla and Lynette.

Marcella then told Angela that she would not want to be put in that position and given those unnecessary tasks.

"And neither will Camilla. She'll get pissed off and leave."

"You think so?"

Angela smiled: *"It worked for Ms. Henderson."*

"I needed to hear that." Marcella smiled and said.

The waiter then walked up and put their tickets on the table.

After paying, they left.

"I'll call and let you know what happens," Marcella told her as they were getting in their cars.

Chapter – Twenty-nine

DECEPTION OF INCREASE REVEALED

A ***week later,*** Marcella called and told Angela that Camilla and Lynette had been hired. Camilla was assigned the job as Ms. Fuller's assistant, and Lynette was hired as assistant manager with the elderly transportation services.

Camilla had to drive 124 miles round trip each day, and Lynette was driving 112 miles round trip. While working in Birmingham, they would call family and friends throughout the day, but their new job locations were long-distance, and they had to use payphones. The two had previously enjoyed other benefits, such as full-paid health and life insurance, but in their new jobs, they had to pay part of the cost for those benefits. They also lost their membership with the state retirement system because their employers were not eligible for membership. Their wages were far less than they had previously made. In other words, they lost out on many benefits they had previously enjoyed.

After hearing the news about their hiring, Clara called Angela to find out if she had heard. Being inquisitive, Angela called her contacts at the State Commission on Aging and the State Transportation Department. She learned from her contacts that neither state agency had given money for the hiring. Angela and her contacts concluded that perhaps, some wealthy Republican Scott County resident had again put up the money.

Several days later, Angela learned that upon reporting to work, Camilla was given a desk in an open area where Ms. Fuller could see every move she made. She had been assigned the task of sorting and organizing all the records. This was a horrendous task, and Camilla saw it as very demeaning. Knowing Camilla was not pleased, Ms. Fuller constantly checked on her and told her she was the best person for the job. Angela had given them copies of everything they were entitled to; the problem was the order in which she had packed the boxes.

One month after the hiring, the COA financial officer scheduled a training meeting for Ms. Fuller, her bookkeeper, and her secretary. Upon hearing about the upcoming meeting, Councilwoman Jones and Commissioner Hudson decided to invite others in to hear firsthand how much better off the aging program would be. They then took it upon themselves to invite the news media, the pull-out team members, the county coordinators, members of the non-profit boards they came under, and other interested citizens.

Councilwoman Jones and Commissioner Hudson were excited and looking forward to the training meeting. Their ego led them to believe that the information they would receive at the meeting would show that the pull-out team's fight to take the program had not been in vain. They were under the impression that the COA financial officer would confirm what they had bragged about.

During the hearings to take the program, a state board member had told them that they had not considered all the odds. However, they could not believe that their actions would not significantly benefit them. To prove they were right, they wanted all the people to hear for themselves, about the increase in funding. They had promised to be open and truthful about the agency's finances, and this was their opportunity to live up to their promises. Sadly, to say, they would later regret having so many witnesses.

On the day of the training meeting when the COA team, Wilson and his assistant Melinda arrived, they were escorted to a large conference room. Upon seeing all the people, Wilson thought that maybe they were in the wrong location. As he and Melinda were about to leave, Councilwoman Jones came over to greet them. She told them that she had invited all the people so they could hear firsthand how much better off financially the program was going to be. She went on to say that they had promised to do things differently than the Planning Commission had done. Councilwoman Jones then introduced Wilson and Melinda to the attendees, telling them that Wilson was there to provide training. She then gave Wilson and Melinda copies of the information sheets she was planning to talk about. Being taken by surprise Wilson nor Melinda commented. Considering there were no written programs, he had no idea as to how things would be carried out or what Councilwoman Jones was thinking they would say.

Councilwoman Jones and Cheryl had laid out an assortment of refreshments for the occasion. Before the meeting started, everyone was talking and enjoying themselves. The county coordinators appeared very jubilant as they talked about what they planned to do with the increased funding they were expecting. Despite the fact the County Commissioners from Butler and Woodrow County had told their county coordinators not to expect an increase, they were still hopeful. Marcella was also thinking that maybe they would all be getting extra funds, even after Angela had told her that the funds were not in the grant.

Their thinking was based on the fact that the Scott County Commission had provided the new aging agency with all its needs, such as space, furniture, equipment, utilities, telephone services, and supplies.

As they waited to get started, Councilwoman Jones proudly walked around, greeting everyone and thanking them for coming. She was telling them that this was the day they had been fighting for. Meanwhile, Wilson and Melinda sat quietly, waiting and watching. Like so many others, they had also been reading the newspapers and had heard all the talk about the big financial increases the counties would get. They thought that maybe the wealthy Republican citizens who had bailed the agency out twice were giving the county programs a large donation.

Finally, the meeting got started. Councilwoman Jones and Cheryl passed out copies of the information documents. Wilson and Melinda had already begun reviewing the copies they had been given earlier and were wondering why the Planning Commission budget summary pages were included. As Councilwoman Jones talked, Melinda whispered to Wilson, *"I hope she's not thinking these are aging program dollars."*

"I hope not, but we'll soon find out."

While everyone was looking at their sheets, Councilwoman Jones started explaining what was on the pages. She instructed everyone to look at the Planning Commission summary pages. As they looked, she proceeded to go over the figures. It was easy to see the large dollar amounts that she had highlighted.

"Oh no! I can't believe this," Wilson whispered to Melinda, *"She's thinking these are aging program dollars."*

As Councilwoman Jones continued talking, it became apparent to Wilson that she had been led to believe they could divide the figures on the bottom line by five, showing that each county would get the same amount of money.

During their fight to take the program, they had rejected the guidelines that showed how federal and state dollars were allocated. Angela had told them on several occasions that the money was allocated based on various factors. However, it was easy for Wilson to see that Councilwoman Jones and the pull-out team members had rejected those factors.

Hearing all the incorrect information being presented, Melinda wanted to speak out, but Wilson decided to let Councilwoman Jones continue giving out false information. Finally, after she had gone on for a while, Wilson decided it was time to stop her. *"Councilwoman Jones,"* he said, *"Melinda and I want to know how you came up with the $150,000 you're showing each county will get."*

His statement got the attention of the attendees. As they looked on, waiting for Councilwoman Jones to respond, she hesitated for a moment, then proudly instructed them to look at the Planning Commission budget sheets.

"No! No! No! You got it wrong." Wilson said. *"Those are not aging program dollars."*

Wilson's statement stunned the attendees, and they began raising their hands to ask for clarification. Knowing the confusion his statement had created, Wilson apologized for interrupting and then began explaining the information on the Planning Commission budget sheets. He told them they were looking at budget summary pages. He went on to say that the former AAA Director administered several large pass-through grants and the figures they were looking at were a combination of several grants. He explained that the figures they were looking at covered all the costs relating to the employees hired under the grants, in addition to the grant administrator's expense.

He then said, *"While I'm on the subject, I would like to clear up a few other things, you have been misled about."*

He went on to talk about the expenses covered under the indirect cost category. He pointed out that all of those expenses were necessary and could be eliminated when operating a program. He said, while listening, he was trying to figure out how Councilwoman Jones had come up with the $150,000. But after dividing the bottom line by five it became clear to him. He then looked around the room and said. *"I'm sorry, but those figures do not represent aging program dollars."*

He then looked at Councilwoman Jones and Commissioner Hudson and said, *"You're giving out money that's not in the aging program grant."*

It was apparent they were all stunned, as they looked on shaking their heads in dismay. One of the reporters then raised his hand to ask a question. He wanted to know where Councilwoman Jones had gotten her information from. Wilson then pointed to Councilwoman Jones so she could answer the question. Not wanting to reveal her informant, Councilwoman Jones tried to change the subject. She told the reporter that Wilson would prefer to talk to her privately about that.

"No," Wilson interrupted and said. *"You can answer the reporter's question."*

It was apparent that she did not wish to respond. Wilson then told the attendees that it was obvious that pull-out team members had been lied to. One of the reporters then asked; *"Why do you think they had been given misleading information?"*

Wilson let out a short chuckle then said; *"To make them believe they would be better off financially when they pulled from under the Planning Commission."*

Hearing the statement, they all sat looking dumbfounded. One of Commissioner Hudson's counterparts, who had walked in while Wilson was talking, asked Wilson to reiterate what he had said about the Planning Commission budget summary pages. Wilson took the time to repeat some of the things he had said moments earlier. The commissioner also wanted to know why Ms. Marshall was managing the various state grants. Wilson explained, stating that when a state agency wanted to implement a new program, they were required to go through the state personnel system to hire workers. However sometimes, realizing the time involved, and the urgency to implement the program the state agencies would solicit the aid of an outside contractor. The contracting agency would write up a plan that covers all the costs involved in administering the program and the state department would enter into a contract agreement to pay all those costs.

He again chuckled and said; *"While the fight to take the aging program was going, Ms. Marshall was writing grant proposals and entering into contracts with various state, city, and county agencies."*

"That was smart of her." One of the reporters said.

Another person asked: *"How many contracts does she have?"*

"That I don't know," Wilson said.

Considering the time they had spent dealing with issues unrelated to the purpose of their mission, Wilson then took out the budget sheets he had brought and asked Ms. Fuller if she would allow her secretary to make copies. After returning and passing out the copies, Wilson instructed them to look at the sheets he had brought. Each page had a title showing the types of funds and the purpose of the funds. He explained the information on each sheet, pointing to the amount of money awarded by the Commission of Aging and the funding sources of the money. He told them that the counties would get less money than they had gotten while with the Planning Commission. His statement shocked everyone in the room, and they started asking specific questions to understand why.

Seeing the figures listed as in-kind dollars, one of the individuals raised her hand and asked Wilson to explain. Wilson explained that in-kind was a non-monetary contribution such as the cost of goods, services, and time, paid by someone to cover the expense of another. He used the example of all the goods and services Scott County Commission was providing to QC-AAA.

Then all of a sudden Clara spoke out after coming to an understanding of all the information Wilson was providing. She told the other attendees that Ms. Marshall had tried to get them to understand that they would not get any more money, but greed had taken control, and they didn't believe her.

"*I'm sorry,*" Wilson said. "*It's apparent someone has played a con game on y'all.*"

"*I can't believe this,*" Clara yelled. "*I told Juanita several days ago I was in it for the money.*"

Melinda then said, "*Well… there is no more money. As Wilson said, each of you will end up getting less.*"

"*How much less?*" One of the reporters asked.

"*The AAA will get the same administrative funds other AAAs get,*" Wilson told them. "*Ms. Fuller will be much better off because Scott County has agreed to cover many of the expenses the AAA would normally have to pay for.*"

He went on to say that the counties would get less based on various factors.

"*Can you give an estimate?*" One of the reporters asked.

Wilson went on to explain that the amount they received would depend on the number of clients they served.

Clara then stood up and pointed at Councilwoman Jones and the County Commissioners, "*Y'all were so determined to take the program; you lied and falsified reports to gain our trust.*"

She went on to say that Councilwoman Jones, Susan, and the Scott County Commissioners had Clair County Commissioners believing that the Planning Commission was misappropriating the aging program dollars. As she continued talking, she said that Susan and her supporters had lied, filling their heads with beliefs that they would financially benefit by pulling from under the Planning Commission. As Clara talked, no one said a word. From the sound of her voice, it was apparent she was distraught. She then looked around the room and said to the other county coordinators, *"Y'all don't have to say anything; we had it good with the Planning Commission."*

At that point, Councilwoman Jones attempted to dismiss the media, telling them that the COA Financial team would be more comfortable if they were not present. Wilson quickly spoke out and told the reporters he was okay with them staying.

Realizing the time they had spent dealing with misinformation, Wilson suggested to Ms. Fuller that they move to another location without the presence of non-essential people.

Immediately after getting back to her office, Marcella called Angela and asked if they could meet, so she could tell her what went on at the meeting. From the sound of Marcella's voice, Angela could sense that Marcella needed to talk. But unfortunately, Angela was too busy working on proposals she needed to take to Montgomery the following day. Wanting to hear what Marcella would tell her, Angela suggested they meet for lunch the following day.

As promised, on her way back Angela stopped off at Shoney's to meet with Marcella. Having seen excerpts of news reports of the meeting, Angela knew things had not gone as many had expected. Angela was now looking forward to hearing what Marcella would tell her. As she approached the table, she could tell from the look on Marcella's face that she was not a happy camper.

"Well," Angela said as she was taking a seat.

"Angela, you'll never believe what happened."

At that moment, the waiter came over to take their order. Considering they were known, frequent customers, the three chatted briefly. After the waiter had walked away, Marcella started telling Angela about the things that had gone on at the meeting. She told Angela practically every detail. As Angela listened, she could visualize having been present. After they had talked for nearly two hours they said goodbye and Angela left.

Chapter – Thirty

SEARCHING FOR MORE INCOME

After the training meeting with COA, and learning of the short-fall in funding, the county coordinators realized that they would not be getting the increase in funding they had hoped for. However, realizing that the AAA funds had not decreased, and Scott County Commissioners were taking care of practically all of the AAA's overhead expenses, Cheryl and Clara began asking the AAA for more money.

Believing Camilla was indebted to them, Cheryl and Councilwoman Jones thought that maybe Camilla could tell them how Ms. Fuller was spending the money. Suspecting that Camilla may have been communicating with the two and providing information, Ms. Fuller decided to keep everything from Camilla. To keep her other staff informed, Ms. Fuller would hold meetings with them on days she had sent Camilla to the field. Knowing she was being kept in the dark and couldn't do anything about it created a great deal of stress for Camilla.

Camilla's husband was outraged, that she had gotten herself in so much trouble she could no longer handle their family affairs. Having to deal with problems at home and on the job was very stressful. After being on the job for less than five months Camilla left work one after-noon, drove home, picked up her children, and left town without telling anyone.

As time passed, everything at the Planning Commission seemed to be going well. Even though Angela had been told she would always have a job, she knew it depended on her bringing in contracts. Having earlier foreseen the probability of losing the aging program, she had completed grant proposals that had been approved. The grants were much larger with more contract workers. They were bringing in money that increased the Commission's overall budget. However, it was pass-through money that could not be used to replace the loss of funds, the aging program had paid into the in-direct cost pool. Other than Angela, the only other staff members who benefited were the accountant, account clerk, secre-taries, receptionist, and Mr. Percy, and theirs' was based on the number of hours they performed work relating to the contracts.

One afternoon after some time had passed, Angela was working on time sheets when Valeria walked in. As usual, she had a big smile on her face. It was apparent something positive had occurred. Valeria immedi-ately announced that she had gotten a job closer to home. Angela was elated to hear the good news, for she and Valeria had often sat in the park and prayed, asking God to give Valeria employment closer to her home. Not only had God answered their prayers, but God was giving Valeria more than she had expected. Two weeks later, the staff was celebrating with Valeria and wishing her farewell.

After Valeria left, the programs she had administered were trans-ferred under Angela's management. Angela was managing the Medicaid Waiver Program, Senior Employment Program, and ten large pass-through employment services contracts. Administering the Senior Employment Program put Angela in a position of having to again deal with the county coordinators. Each county aging program had five to seven senior workers working with them as cooks, kitchen helpers, cen-ter managers, homemakers, transportation aid, etc. Working with the county coordinators, Angela tried to avoid any unnecessary chatter about the problems they were going through.

Having many contract workers assigned to other county agencies, Angela frequently visited those agencies. During her visits, the agency directors and supervisors were always telling her about the aging program problems that were written up in the newspapers.

During that time, there was hardly a day that went by without something being written in the newspaper about the financial difficulties the aging programs were going through. Reading about all the negative things, Scott County citizens were outraged. They held weekly meetings to discuss getting rid of the Republican County Commissioners. When interviewed, the citizens expressed their anger, stating that they couldn't believe the county commissioners had stooped so low as to allow Councilwoman Jones and Susan to get them in so much trouble.

The newspapers in the five counties wrote articles about the aging programs' financial troubles. They stated that each county program had taken cuts in funding ranging from $25K to $35K. In addition to those cuts in funding, the county programs were having to take on expenses they had not anticipated. While with the Planning Commission, the AAA had included in the Commission's Insurance Plan, coverage for the counties' 18-passenger transportation vans. The county programs were now having to obtain their coverage at a much higher cost.

As time passed, Ms. Fuller was faced with many difficulties. Clara and Cheryl were constantly asking for more money. They were still convinced that the money was available because Ms. Fuller did not have to pay for overhead and other related common expenses. To avoid the pressure they were imposing on her, Ms. Fuller decided to stop dealing with them and start dealing with the heads of the non-profit boards their programs came under. That forced Cheryl and Clara to have to go to their board chairman, who then had to go to Ms. Fuller to obtain the information needed. This was an uncomfortable task for the men who served as board chairman. The non-profits had been established as shelters for the aging programs and not as real management boards. The responsibilities imposed on the senior citizens who served on those boards were a bit too much.

Councilwoman Jones was another problem Ms. Fuller had to deal with. Having previously served as the chairman of the non-profit board the Scott County Aging Program came under, Councilwoman Jones was still trying to hold on to power. She was always sneaking around, asking questions, and trying to tell Ms. Fuller and the Scott County Aging Program non-profit board chairman how to run the programs. Ms. Fuller's refusal to accept Councilwoman Jones's suggestions created a great deal of conflict between them. To avoid conflict, Ms. Fuller decided to put Councilwoman Jones in the category of being an adversary.

As time passed, county residents being aware of the money problems issues and knowing the county commissioners were responsible for the changes, believed the county commissioners should be held accountable for the financial shortfalls.

The write-ups in the newspaper's editorial column always criticized the county commissioners for their bad decisions. In addition, news reporters were interviewing county residents who told them they would be going to the polls during the election and making their feelings known.

During the same period, information about how well the Planning Commission was doing was also covered in the newspapers. The news focused on the programs the Planning Commission was still administering. During interviews with reporters, Mr. Percy bragged a great deal about the money the programs were bringing in. He told the reporters that losing the aging program had not caused the devastation to the Commission many had expected.

In addition to the articles in the newspaper, the Planning Commission's quarterly newsletters highlighted all the good things that were going on. The cost of the publications and the mail-outs was more than $25K quarterly. On numerous occasions, the Commission Executive Committee members had strongly advised Mr. Percy to reduce the cost by decreasing the amount of information put in the publications and the number of publications printed and mailed out. However, Mr. Percy failed to take their advice; he wanted everyone to know just how great the Planning Commission was doing.

After taking the aging program, Republican County Commissioners from Scott and Clair County stopped attending the Commission

Executive Committee meetings. However, they did send in a proxy. After reading about all the good things going on at the Planning Commission, they started coming back. Mr. Percy was elated to see them and took it upon himself to let them know that their actions had not stopped the Commissions from providing services to the elderly. He arrogantly boasted about the success of the waiver program and the money it was bringing in. Hearing him brag caused the Scott and Clair County Commissioners to conclude that the waiver program was the missing piece of the puzzle that was causing financial shortfalls for the newly established aging program. After one of the executive committee meetings, Commissioner Elmore approached Mr. Percy and told him that the Republican County Commissioners were going to the Governor to ask to have the waiver program given to the QC-AAA.

At that time more than twelve months had passed since the transfer of the aging program. The county commissioners thought that getting the waiver program would solve their financial problems. Since taking the aging program, they had to put more money into the county aging program budgets to keep the programs operating.

To avoid another battle, a group of Aging Program County Commissioners went to the Governor with their request. Six weeks later, Mr. Percy received a letter from COA notifying him that they would be transferring the waiver program to QC-AAA. The transfer date was five weeks away. Mr. Percy was devastated; he had not foreseen this coming. He began talking to executive committee members about the financial problems it would pose for the Commission if they lost the waiver program. However, none of them seemed to have cared. When Mr. Percy continued complaining about losing the program, Commissioner Elmore confronted him and told him he would have him fired if he spoke another word about losing the program.

During the weeks to come, the Commission Executive Committee members remained relatively quiet about losing the program. It was said that the county commissioners were thinking that the waiver program would save their county governments from having to continue supporting their county aging programs. Though it was never confirmed, it was believed that all of the county commissioners had agreed to take the waiver program from the Commission.

Upon learning about the upcoming transfer, the Medicaid Waiver clients and their family members did not take it quietly; they expressed their concerns. They talked about the big mistake the state aging board had made when they took the aging program and the financial disaster that had been brought on.

When the media heard about the upcoming transfer of the program, they went out and interviewed the clients and family members. The reporters were told that the county commissioners were trying to find money to make up for the shortfalls the county aging programs were going through. The reporters then met with Commissioner Hudson and Councilwoman Jones. The two admitted that they had failed to realize the cost-effectiveness of having both the Title III Aging and the waiver program. When the reporters asked them to explain how the waiver program would solve the aging program's financial problems, they began bragging. They told the reporters that the county aging programs and the AAA would be financially better off after getting the program. Unfortunately, neither Councilwoman Jones nor Commissioner Hudson knew the usage guidelines. They didn't realize that the guidelines would prohibit the AAA from using the funds for purposes other than those outlined in the federal guidelines. They were presuming that the waiver program would provide the county aging programs with additional funding.

When the COA State Board members read the newspapers, several of them called Angela to obtain information about funding usage. Angela provided them with all the federal and state regulations. Realizing the financial difficulties that had come about after taking the aging program, several state board members met with Angela to write up some usage standards.

The AAA was to continue providing the same services outlined by the case managers. They were to retain the existing case managers and service providers and pay them the same wages. The AAA was prohibited from using the waiver funding for purposes not stimulated in federal regulations. These constraints eliminated the AAA's ability to use the funds to alleviate the financial problems the counties were going through.

Two weeks before the scheduled date of transfer, the question of where the program would be housed became an issue. The AAA space was not large enough to accommodate the waiver program materials and staff. With all the space in that county building already taken, Ms. Fuller was faced with having to locate and rent space. When state board members learned about the space problem, they went to Scott County Commissioners and told them they had to live up to their pledge of providing the needed accommodations. The Republican County Commissioners then gave the AAA additional space in the same building. Their decision required relocating some of the county services to other buildings. The problem was the other buildings were older than the newly built building they were in. The staff providing those services was furious, and they complained. The county commissioner's decision resulted in a great deal of adverse publicity and animosity from employees and county residents. When the newspaper reporters got wind of the animosity, they talked with the employees and county residents. The reporters were told that the county commissioners seemed to have forgotten they were voters and the election date would be coming up.

After the transfer of the waiver program, Ms. Fuller, her bookkeeper, and her secretary received salary increases. When the word about the salary increases got out, Cheryl and Clara were livid. They went to their board chairman, but they were unable to get any help.

Chapter – Thirty-one

CONSEQUENCES OF GREED

Having lost their fight for more funding, the county coordinators thought they had nothing more to fight for. Unfortunately, they were unaware that the most significant battle was yet to come. They were unaware that the State Commission on Aging was putting a great deal of pressure on Ms. Fuller to persuade her to join the statewide meals contract. The constant pressure and the complaints coming from the county coordinators resulted in the QC-AAA Board's decision to eliminate the problem by joining the statewide meals contract. At that time the QC-AAA was approaching three years of being in existence. The action the AAA had taken came as a devastating blow to the county coordinators, for they had never envisioned this would come about. Losing the on-site prepared meals program resulted in the closing of the county kitchens and a decrease in the number of seniors who came in daily for their noonday meal. In light of their meals program being the most significant program they administered, losing the program meant they no longer needed ninety-five percent of the people who worked for the programs, many of whom were senior workers who came under the senior employment program Angela administered. No longer needing the workers, Angela immediately reassigned the senior workers to other county agencies.

During Angela's monitoring visits to those agencies, the agency directors and supervisors were always sharing information with her. They would keep copies of news articles written about the problems the aging programs were going through. Angela was also getting her information from those who were being affected. Despite the problems Angela had gone through with Clara and Cheryl, they had maintained a friendly relationship. The two were always calling to fill Angela in on everything that was going on. Their conversations would always start with a question. *"Have you read the Newspapers?"* Regardless of her answer, they would proceed to tell her everything that was going on. They would also acknowledge that they had been lied to by Camilla and Susan, making them believe that they would be better off financially.

Reading about all the negative things occurring, the citizens could easily see that taking the programs had not turned out as had been expected. With all the negative information being talked about, the residents in three of the five counties began pointing fingers. They blamed their Republican County Commissioners, the county coordinators, the COA Deputy Director, and Councilwoman Jones for all the problems.

The Scott County Republican County Commissioners started pulling away from Councilwoman Jones and blaming her for all the problems. However, that did not help them because Scott and Clara County citizens had already begun their campaign to vote their county commissioners out of office. Weekly, articles were written in the newspapers inviting county residents to come to the county commissioners' meetings to witness an open exhibition of political corruption. Scott County residents believed that the best way to solve their problems was to vote the three power-hungry Republican County Commissioners out of office. Large numbers of Scott and Clara County residents started attending the county commissioners' meetings to talk about the chaos the Republican Commissioners had put their county in.

During the time Scott County's three Republican County Commissioners' were in office, they had caused many problems that kept county officials in courts, fighting battles they had brought on. Having been forewarned that they would be voted out of office, the three county commissioners created county jobs for themselves. As time passed, the citizens kept their promise, on the day of the election, the citizens went to voting polls in record numbers. Shortly after the new Scott County Commissioners took office, they did away with the jobs their predecessors had created.

As time passed reading the newspapers and seeing all the changes taking place. Angela was utterly amazed.

Three years after leaving the Planning Commission and going to work with the Cook/Scott Area Transportation Program, Lynette was terminated. Angela was told that she had been terminated due to her inability to come to work on time and put in a full day's work. Knowing of some of the issues she had gone through after leaving the Commission, many people began speculating. Lynette had gone through a nasty divorce and one of her children had been involved in a near-death accident.

Around the same time, former Clair County Commissioner Elmore had lost his life while working in his pasture. The article reported that Mr. Elmore was driving his tractor when one of his cattle ran out in front. To avoid hitting the animal, he turned quickly causing the tractor to overturn and crushing him underneath. The article went on the read that he had served a four-year term as a county commissioner, but was not reelected due to some decisions he made that resulted in the voters deciding not to give him another chance.

Though it was not part of the newspaper article, but, while serving as one of the Planning Commission Executive Committee Members, Commissioner Elmore had caused many problems in his effort to be a good Republican. His decisions caused harm to many people in Clair County who had held him in high regard. He had played a major role in taking the aging programs and the Medicaid Waiver Program from the Planning Commission. His actions resulted in the beginning of the downfall and dismantling of the Clair County Aging Program.

Several weeks later, on her way to a meeting being held at the Commission on Aging, when Angela pulled up to the window of the parking attendant she was taken aback to see Susan. She wondered why Susan was there and not one of the clerical workers. After Susan had given her a sticker for her window, they chatted very briefly and Angela drove away. After getting into the building and passing the door to Susan's former office, she wondered. Later while sitting in the conference room waiting for the meeting to start, one of her counterparts whispered telling her that Susan was no longer the Deputy Director and that she had been dismissed. At that point, Angela was very curious, but, by that time others had come into the room and they could not talk. Angela then whispered, *"Call and tell me what happened."*

Several days later Cheryl called and gave Angela the news. She said Susan had been dismissed because of the problems she had caused, and the downfall and dismantling of the county aging programs.

Three and a half years, after the aging program had been taken, Mr. Percy was dismissed. One Monday morning, when Angela got to work and went to his office to share some information, to her surprise all of the pictures that once hung on his walls had been taken down. She was later told that the executive committee had allowed him to remain until the end of the fiscal year. They had instructed him not to perform any major Commission business, but, unfortunately, something went wrong and they immediately terminated him.

Three weeks later, the Commission, Executive Committee hired a new executive director. After getting to know the staff and reviewing all the policies, he was surprised to see that Angela's salary was considerably less than her male counterparts. Comparing the length of time she had been with the agency and the size of the programs she was administering, being a fair-minded man, he brought the issue to the attention of the executive committee. The executive committee hired an organization to conduct a salary study of individuals performing jobs similar to the job Angela was performing. The study resulted in a sizeable salary increase and a re-classification of Angela's job title.

In 1993 Governor Hanson was removed from office when a grand jury indicted him for theft, conspiracy, and ethics violations. He was convicted for misusing campaign and inaugural funds to pay personal debts.

During his time in office, many people were negatively affected by some of his decisions. He took state-funded programs from democratic-based counties and placed the programs in counties that had voted for him. After Governor Hanson was removed from office the new governor replaced several of the state cabinet commissioners. Commissioner, Rucker of COA was among them. After his dismissal, the incoming Governor appointed a woman to serve as COA Commissioner.

In 1996, Ms. Fuller lost her job, after Scott County's five-year pledge had ended and QC-AAA had moved to Cook County, unlike the deal Scott County had given to the AAA, Cook County did not provide financial support. Being unable to meet program financial needs, Ms. Fuller had used Medicaid Waiver dollars to help cover overhead expenses. During a federal audit, the financial problems were discovered.

After Ms. Fuller's termination, the QC-AAA Board hired Ms. Monroe. Ms. Monroe was tasked to dismantle the county aging program structures which had existed for more than twenty-five years. Ms. Monroe's first move was a splendid one; she started dismantling the Scott County Aging Program by taking all the aging services the county coordinator was still holding on to. Though attempts to fight were made, the county coordinator never had a chance since all of the former county commissioners had been voted out of office.

Ms. Monroe's next move was Clair and Cook County. Dismantling the two-county aging programs was relatively easy, for she had no resistance. The dismantling of the aging programs in the three counties' resulted in getting each of the municipalities in which the senior centers were located to accept the responsibilities of management. However, Ms. Monroe faced significant barriers when she got to the two counties that had held out on being taken. The obstacles she faced resulted in the partial dismantling of those county programs.

In Butler County, unlike the other four counties, the aging program came under the county government, instead of a non-profit organization. The county government paid all the expenses of the senior centers located in the various municipalities. When Ms. Monroe approached the governing officials in those municipalities, the mayors and town council members were unwilling to take on the finance and management responsibilities.

In Woodrow County, Ms. Monroe ran into other problems where the governing officials of the small municipalities were unwilling to take on the financial responsibilities of supporting the senior centers. To accomplish her mission of dismantling the program, Ms. Monroe had their 16-passenger transportation vans taken out of service to force their hand. This resulted in decreases in participation. The seniors who did not have transportation could no longer get to the centers. Another obstacle Ms. Monroe faced was two of the senior centers were located in affluent communities in newly built community buildings that housed a variety of other services and social programs. The seniors who attended those centers were there to socialize and participate in the other activities offered.

Ms. Monroe found that dismantling the Woodrow County Aging Program was far more complicated than she had anticipated. However, after months of negotiating, Ms. Monroe was successful in reaching an agreement. The county aging program coordinator remained as county coordinator overseeing and managing all the senior centers.

Despite the many problems Angela had gone through she felt blessed and vindicated. Being a woman with strong Christian faith, she firmly believed in Romans 8:28, *for we know that all things work together for good to those who love God, to those who are the called according to His purpose.'*

When talking to her friends about the problems her adversaries had faced Angela would sometimes quote Psalms 37:35, *"I have seen the wicked in great power spreading himself like a native green tree. Yet he passed away, and behold; he was no more.'*

In June 2006, Angela gave notice of her decision to retire on December 31, 2006. After her retirement date announcement was publicized, she got many calls from friends and colleagues who joked about her being the last one standing. During one of her conversations with Juanita, the Woodrow County Coordinator, they laughed and joked about things that had gone on over the years. Juanita being aware that several attempts had been made to bring the aging programs back under the Commission, asked Angela how she felt about it. Angela told her that being over those programs was like being in a bad marriage. She was always going through struggles trying to keep them. She went on to say that wise people don't get back into a bad marriage once they have gotten out. Angela told Juanita that having them acknowledge they had been tricked into believing lies and asking her to help them bring the programs back under the Planning Commission was the most gratifying words she could have heard. She went on to say that before being appointed AAA many attempts had been made to take that program, but they had all failed. It was simply a game of power play for those county officials. They had to prove they could beat the big city, educated officials. However, the saddest part was watching good people being destroyed because of greed. In sharing her story with others, Angela would say;

"Strange but true, I outlasted three executive directors and watched all of my adversaries defeated, by the words of God, written in Deuteronomy 20:4, For the Lord your God is He who goes with you to fight for you against your enemies, to give you the victory.

Acronyms – Grasping for Power

AGS	-	Alabama Gerontological Society
AAA	-	Area Agency on Aging
COG	-	Council of Government
JCOSCA	-	Jefferson County Office of Senior Citizens Activities
MSA	-	MS Senior America
MW	-	Medicaid Waiver
OSCA	-	Office of Senior Citizens Activities
PC	-	Planning Commission
POA	-	Program on Aging
QC-AAA	-	Quinary Counties – Area Agency on Aging
RPC	-	Regional Planning Commission
SEP	-	Senior Employment Program
SCOA	-	State Commission on Aging
SW	-	Senior Worker

Made in the USA
Columbia, SC
19 November 2023

26723064R00136